INDIA: 55 MUST SEE PLACES & 50 MUST DO THINGS

Destination Infinity

India: 55 Must See Places & 50 Must Do Things

Table of Contents

Introduction ... 6

India: 55 Must See Places

North India

1. Taj Mahal, Uttar Pradesh ... 11
2. India Gate, Delhi ... 12
3. Qutub Minar, Delhi ... 13
4. Red Fort, Delhi ... 14
5. Humayun's Tomb, Delhi ... 15
6. Mughal Gardens, Jammu & Kashmir ... 16
7. Thikse Monastery, Jammu & Kashmir ... 17
8. Fatehpur Sikri, Uttar Pradesh ... 18
9. Nanda Devi and Valley of Flowers, Uttarakhand ... 19
10. Agra Fort, Uttar Pradesh ... 20
11. Golden Temple, Punjab ... 21
12. Keoladeo National Park, Rajasthan ... 22
13. Chittorgarh Fort, Rajasthan ... 23
14. Jaisalmer Fort, Rajasthan ... 24
15. Jantar Mantar, Rajasthan/Delhi ... 25

South India

1. Meenakshi Amman Temple, Tamil Nadu ... 27
2. Airavatesvara Temple, Tamil Nadu ... 28
3. Gangai-Konda-Cholapuram, Tamil Nadu ... 29
4. Brihadeeswarar Temple, Tamil Nadu ... 30
5. Pancha Rathas, Tamil Nadu ... 31
6. Shore Temple, Tamil Nadu ... 32

7. Kai-la-sa-nadhar Temple, Tamil Nadu … 33
8. Silent Valley National Park, Kerala … 34
9. Mattancherry Palace & Paradesi Synagogue, Kerala … 35
10. Vittala Temple, Karnataka … 36
11. Pattadakal, Karnataka … 37
12. Shravanabelagola, Karnataka … 38
13. Churches of Old Goa, Goa … 39
14. Golkonda Fort, Telangana … 40
15. Qutb Shahi Tombs, Telangana … 41

West & Central India

1. Gwalior Fort, Madhya Pradesh … 43
2. Khajuraho, Madhya Pradesh … 44
3. Mandu Group of Monuments, Madhya Pradesh … 45
4. Orchha, Madhya Pradesh … 46
5. Sanchi Stupa, Madhya Pradesh … 47
6. Chhtrapati Shivaji Terminus, Maharashtra … 48
7. Elephanta Caves, Maharashtra … 49
8. Ajanta Caves, Maharashtra … 50
9. Ellora Caves, Maharashtra … 51
10. Gir Forest & National Park, Gujarat … 53
11. Champaner-Pavagadh, Gujarat … 54
12. Rani ki vav, Gujarat … 55
13. Somnath Temple, Gujarat … 57

East India

1. Bhitarkanika National Park, Odisha … 59
2. Konark Sun Temple, Odisha … 60
3. Mahabodhi Temple, Bihar … 61
4. Sher Shah Suri Tomb, Bihar … 63
5. Neora Valley National Park, West Bengal … 64
6. Shantiniketan, West Bengal … 65
7. Sundarbans National Park, West Bengal … 66
8. Bishnupur Temples, West Bengal … 68
9. Victoria Memorial, West Bengal … 69
10. Kaziranga National Park, Assam … 70

11. Majuli River Island, Assam … 71
12. Manas National Park, Assam … 72
13. Namdapha National Park, Arunachal Pradesh … 74
14. Khangchendronga National Park, Sikkim … 75

India: 50 Must Do Things

1. See a Bollywood/Regional Language Movie … 78
2. Eat Indian Sweets & Savories … 81
3. Listen to Indian (Popular) Music … 83
4. Drink Indian Tea … 85
5. Eat Chat Items … 87
6. Glance through a newspaper … 89
7. Eat Indian breakfast … 91
8. Travel in a Train … 93
9. Eat Indian Fruits/Drink Fruit Juices … 95
10. Wear traditional Indian clothes … 97
11. Visit a place of worship … 99
12. Eat the Biryani … 101
13. Drink Milk products (Butter-milk, Lassi,...) … 103
14. Drink/Eat Tender Coconut … 105
15. Buy (and wear) Accessories … 107
16. Go for a Lion/Tiger safari … 109
17. Ride an Elephant/Camel … 111
18. Buy Jewelery … 113
19. Attend an Indian wedding … 115
20. Eat the Indian bread – Roti/Chapati … 116
21. Apply Mehndi … 118
22. Attend Music Concerts … 119
23. See Indian Dance … 121
24. Listen to Indian musical instruments … 123
25. Visit a Heritage house … 125
26. Get yourself an Ayurvedic Massage/Visit an Ayurvedic Spa … 126
27. Go see a Cricket Match … 128
28. Watch Field Hockey … 130
29. Learn Yoga/Meditation … 132
30. Stick a Bindi on your forehead … 134

31. Read books written by Indian authors … 135
32. Ride in an Auto … 137
33. Drink the Coffee … 139
34. Read/See the Mythological Epic stories – Ramayana & Mahabharata … 141
35. Sponsor a meal in an orphanage and interact with the kids … 143
36. Have an Astrologer predict your future … 144
37. Participate in Indian festivals … 146
38. Drink Lime Soda/Masala Soda … 148
39. See a Peacock … 150
40. Watch domestic animals share the road … 151
41. Take a Tour of the slums … 152
42. Visit the Palaces & Forts … 153
43. Explore the Colonial Heritage structures … 154
44. Visit the Beaches … 155
45. Visit Art Galleries … 157
46. Learn to Cook Indian food … 158
47. Learn an Indian language … 160
48. Indulge in spiritualism … 162
49. Rural Tourism … 164
50. Read Indian Blogs … 165

List of Recommended Services

List of Recommended Services for Tourists Visiting India … 167

Introduction:

This book is not a tourist guide to India. It's a companion guide to a tourist guide, a short reference book for tourists who don't have the time to go through thick tourist guides. This book is also meant for those who are undecided on whether to make that trip to India or not. And if you want to try out the best of what India has to offer without leaving the comfort of your home, this book is for you too.

In the first section, you'll find an introduction to 55 interesting places in India with historical or geographical significance, with pictures. Most of the listed places are UNESCO World Heritage sites, and are organized according to the zone they belong to: North, West, South and East of India.

In the second section, you'll find a list (with a short explanation) of 50 interesting and exciting things to do while you are in India. Most of these activities mentioned are unique to India, but not all of them might be available at every location you visit. It may be better to read about them beforehand, select the ones that appeal to you, and check if those activities are available where you're staying. You might want to keep this book with you while traveling around the country for handy reference.

While I admit that I am no expert in the tourism sector, the locations and activities mentioned in this book are all the ones I'd recommend to a friend traveling from abroad. So they are more of a friendly suggestion than a well-researched & professional list, the purpose being I don't want to drown the reader in a sea of unnecessary information. Thus, this book is perfect if you are on a short tour.

In the third section is given a list of (what I consider to be) the best services you may find useful while in India. For example, if you want to buy a mobile connection, you'll find a short list of recommended and trusted vendors so that you can make your purchases with confidence, without having to look around too much or depend on anyone. This is a general list applicable throughout India, but at certain places you may find better services locally. If you are in doubt, or if these services don't deliver to your location, it's best to check with a local.

I hope you'll enjoy the pictures and the read. Your feedback to improve this work is welcome.

About the author:

Destination Infinity is the online identity of Rajesh K, a professional blogger living in Chennai, India.

When he was young, Rajesh came across a tag-line contest for Indian Tourism. "Destination Infinity" was his creation for that contest, but unfortunately (or fortunately) "Incredible India" won it. As a youngster, he was very angry with the Government for rejecting what he thought was the intellectually superior tag-line. So he decided to make it famous all by himself. All these efforts of blogging and writing eBooks are a result of that youthful streak in him – it just refuses to go away!

"Sustainable-Living" is his latest mantra, but it is not in his style to stick to just one passion. You can catch all his misadventures at his personal blog: www.destinationinfinity.org.

He has also written a novel, "The Archers Revenge", a crime fiction novella set in India.

Copyright:

2nd Edition, India: 55 Must See Places and 50 Must Do Things

Copyright © 2015 by Rajesh K (Destination Infinity)

All rights reserved. This book or any portion thereof may not be reproduced or used in any manner whatsoever without the express written permission of the author except for the use of brief quotations in a book review.

Acknowledgments:

Editor: Anuradha Mehta (anuradhamehta84@gmail.com)

Credit for the photo used on the cover:

By Vinayaraj (Own work) (https://commons.wikimedia.org/wiki/User:Vinayaraj) [CC BY-SA 3.0 (http://creativecommons.org/licenses/by-sa/3.0)], via Wikimedia Commons.

India: 55 Must See Places

North India

1. Taj Mahal, Uttar Pradesh

Let me start with the most popular tourist destination of India – the Taj Mahal, the symbol of eternal love. Constructed using white marble in the 17th Century by Mughal ruler Shah Jahan in the memory of his beloved wife, the Taj Mahal is located in Agra, Uttar Pradesh, North India. It is a UNESCO World Heritage Site and is one of the seven man-made Wonders on Earth. A photo can not really do justice to its beauty and grandeur.

*Photo credit: Dhirad
(https://commons.wikimedia.org/wiki/User:Deep750) [GFDL
(http://www.gnu.org/copyleft/fdl.html), CC-BY-SA-3.0
(http://creativecommons.org/licenses/by-sa/3.0/) or CC-BY-SA-2.0
(http://creativecommons.org/licenses/by-sa/2.0)], via Wikimedia Commons.*

2. India Gate, Delhi

Located in Delhi, North India, the India Gate is a very popular tourist attraction. Built by the British during their rule, it has been renamed 'Amar Jawan Jyoti' or 'Tomb of the Unknown soldier'. This monument is 42 meters high and located inside a hexagonal complex that covers 625 meters.

Photo Credit: Rdglobetrekker (Own work) (https://commons.wikimedia.org/w/index.php?title=User:Rdglobetrekker) [CC-BY-SA-3.0 (http://creativecommons.org/licenses/by-sa/3.0)], via Wikimedia Commons.

3. Qutub Minar, Delhi

The Qutub Minar in Delhi, at 72.5 meters, is one of the oldest and tallest minarets still standing in India. Constructed in the 12th Century and renovated many times, it is a UNESCO World Heritage Site. Did you know that people were allowed to climb to the top of this monument until 1981? Then, a power-cut created a stampede on its narrow stairs and killed 45 people, so it was subsequently closed.

Photo Credit: Krupasindhu Muduli (Own work) (https://commons.wikimedia.org/wiki/User:Krupasindhu_Muduli) [CC-BY-SA-3.0 (http://creativecommons.org/licenses/by-sa/3.0)], via Wikimedia Commons.

4. Red Fort, Delhi

The Red Fort or Lal Qila in Delhi, North India, is another UNESCO World Heritage Site. It was a fort constructed by Shah Jahan in 1648 and remained the main residence of the Mughal emperors until 1857. The red sandstone used extensively on the outer walls gives the fort its name. The ceilings in multiple complexes inside the fort were lined with pure silver, and the famous Peacock Throne & Kohinoor Diamond once adorned the palace. Every year on 15th August, the Prime Minister of India hoists the National Flag and addresses the nation from here.

Photo credit: Shajankumar (Own work) (https://commons.wikimedia.org/w/index.php?title=User:Shajankumar) [CC-BY-SA-3.0 (http://creativecommons.org/licenses/by-sa/3.0)], via Wikimedia Commons.

5. Humayun's Tomb, Delhi

Humayun's Tomb was built along the Yamuna river in 1572, in memory of the Mughal Emperor Humayun, as ordered by his wife Bega Begum. This 47m tall, 91m wide structure was among the first to be built using red sandstone on a large scale. This site was designed as a garden plus tomb, and the tombs of many people of the Mughal empire, including Humayun's favorite barber, can be found here.

Photo credit: Ujjwal India (Own work) (https://commons.wikimedia.org/w/index.php?title=User:Ujjwal_India) [CC-BY-SA-3.0 (http://creativecommons.org/licenses/by-sa/3.0)], via Wikimedia Commons.

6. Mughal Gardens, Jammu & Kashmir

Many Mughal emperors created elaborate gardens in India, especially in Kashmir, after the conceptual model of Persian gardens. These gardens contained a central high-altitude water pool, running water, fountains, other pools, and lots of flora. The two prominent Mughal gardens of Kashmir – Shalimar Bagh & Nishat Bagh – were constructed in the first half of 17th century. They were built as terraced gardens and encompassed an enormous area, and are situated adjoining the beautiful Dal lake.

Photo credit: Vinayaraj (Own work)
(http://commons.wikimedia.org/wiki/User:Vinayaraj) [CC-BY-SA-3.0
(http://creativecommons.org/licenses/by-sa/3.0)], via Wikimedia Commons.

7. Thikse Monastery, Jammu & Kashmir

Thikse is a Tibetian Buddhist Monastery of the Yellow hat (Gelugpa) sect, located at an altitude of 3600m, in Central Ladakh. Established in the 15th century, this is the largest Monastery in this region. The architecture resembles Potala Palace in Lhasa, Tibet – the former seat of the Dalai Lamas – and is 12 stories tall. The top-most floor houses the incarnate Lama of the Monastery. A large pillar engraved with Buddhist teachings is also located here.

Photo credit: Shrikanthhegde (Own work)
(https://commons.wikimedia.org/w/index.php?title=User:Shrikanthhegde)
[CC-BY-SA-3.0 (http://creativecommons.org/licenses/by-sa/3.0)], via Wikimedia Commons.

8. Fatehpur Sikri, Uttar Pradesh

Fatehpur Sikri was founded in 1569 by the Mughal Emperor Akbar. It was the capital of Mughal empire from 1571 to 1585, and is a planned walled-city containing a series of well-preserved palaces, courts, mosques and other utility buildings that offer a fine glimpse into Mughal architecture, which historically combined both Persian and Indian styles. After 1585 it was abruptly abandoned, and hence now resembles a ghost town with many buildings but no inhabitants.

Photo credit: Sanyambahga (Own work) (http://commons.wikimedia.org/wiki/User:Sanyambahga) [CC-BY-SA-3.0 (http://creativecommons.org/licenses/by-sa/3.0)], via Wikimedia Commons.

9. Nanda Devi and Valley of Flowers, Uttarakhand

Both these UNESCO World Heritage sites/National parks are situated 3600 meters and more above sea-level, in the mighty Himalayas. Nanda Devi National Park is situated around the massive snow-clad Nanda Devi peak. The Valley of Flowers, accidentally discovered in 1930s, is situated nearby. Many unique and endangered species of flora and fauna are found in this area, and it also contains a number of rare medicinal plants. Trekking is a very popular activity here.

Photo credit: Pankaj Says So at en.wikipedia [Public domain] (http://en.wikipedia.org/wiki/en:User:Pankaj_Says_So), via Wikimedia Commons.

10. Agra Fort, Uttar Pradesh

The Agra Fort is a UNESCO World Heritage site that covers 3,80,000 sq. m. Plus, 70-feet high boundary walls around the semi-circular site makes it almost like a walled city. Originally built with bricks prior to 10 CE, Emperor Akbar later built it with red sandstone. This Fort was the seat of power for many emperors ruling India, and was its second capital during medieval times. More than 30 uniquely styled Mughal monuments are located here. Agra Fort was also an important site during the 1857 Indian mutiny.

*Photo credit: Jmacleantaylor (Own work)
(https://commons.wikimedia.org/w/index.php?title=User:Jmacleantaylor)
[CC-BY-SA-3.0 (http://creativecommons.org/licenses/by-sa/3.0)], via
Wikimedia Commons.*

11. Golden Temple, Punjab

Harmandir Sahib or the Golden Temple in Amritsar is the holy place of worship in Sikhism (a religion in India). Initially built by the fifth Sikh Guru, Guru Arjan in the 16th Century, it was rebuilt in 18th Century by Jessa Singh Ahluwalia. Maharaja Ranjit Singh later covered the upper floors with gold, from where it got the name 'Golden Temple'. There are four entrances to signify that people of any religion, gender, caste, etc. can visit this shrine. Visitors need to climb down the steps to enter.

Photo credit: Asajaysharma13 (Own work)
(https://commons.wikimedia.org/w/index.php?title=User:Asajaysharma13)
[CC-BY-SA-3.0 (http://creativecommons.org/licenses/by-sa/3.0)], via Wikimedia Commons.

12. Keoladeo National Park, Rajasthan

Keoladeo National Park and Bharatpur Bird Sanctuary are located in Bharatpur in Rajasthan, North India. Did you know that this 29 sq. km National Park for birds was man-made and man-managed? It is one of the biggest avifauna/bird sanctuaries in India, where more than 360 species have been spotted and over 230 species have made their home. It is locally known as Ghana, and is a UNESCO World Heritage site.

Photo credit: rachel dale from new york, ny (peacock Uploaded by Snowmanradio) (http://www.flickr.com/photos/67536509@N00) [CC-BY-SA-2.0 (http://creativecommons.org/licenses/by-sa/2.0)], via Wikimedia Commons.

13. Chittorgarh Fort, Rajasthan

The Chittorgarh Fort was ruled by Chattari Rajputs from 7 CE to 16 CE, and abandoned after that. It was the place where 13,000 women killed themselves in an event called Jauhar, when 30,000 of their men fought and died. They did it because rather than surrender to their enemies during a siege they preferred to die. One of the largest forts in India, it contains many temples, palaces & living quarters. Originally, it had 84 water bodies (fed by natural catchment and rainfall), sufficient to provide for an army of 50,000 for four years! Seven major fortification layers secures this area.

Photo credit: Ssjoshi111 (Own work) (https://commons.wikimedia.org/w/index.php?title=User:Ssjoshi111) [CC-BY-SA-3.0 (http://creativecommons.org/licenses/by-sa/3.0)], via Wikimedia Commons.

14. Jaisalmer Fort, Rajasthan

Jaisalmer Fort is one of the largest forts in the world – it is more than 1 km long and the circumference of the wall is more than 5 km! Built in 1156 CE by the Rajput ruler, Rawal Jaisal, it is located on the top of a small hill in the great Thar desert. There are three layers of walls that protect the fort from enemies and until recent times, the entire population of the city lived inside the fort. Around 500 to 600 thousand tourists visit this fort annually.

Photo credit: Janardanprasad (Own work)
(http://commons.wikimedia.org/wiki/User:Janardanprasad) [CC-BY-SA-3.0
(http://creativecommons.org/licenses/by-sa/3.0)], via Wikimedia Commons.

15. Jantar Mantar, Rajasthan/Delhi

You will find a Jantar Mantar in Jaipur and in Delhi. This is an astronomical observatory built by Raja Jai Singh II between 1724 & 1733. The sites contain a collection of architectural and astronomical instruments built (of stone) to measure time, predict eclipses, the onset, length & duration of local monsoons, and also to track stars in orbits, measure latitudes and longitudes of celestial bodies, and so on. The Samrat Yantra located here is the world's largest sundial with an accuracy of 2 seconds – its shadow moves at 1mm per second and its movement is visible.

Photo credit: Shank (Own work)
(https://commons.wikimedia.org/w/index.php?title=User:Shank) [CC-BY-SA-3.0 (http://creativecommons.org/licenses/by-sa/3.0)], via Wikimedia Commons.

South India

1. Meenakshi Amman Temple, Tamil Nadu

The Meenakshi Amman Temple is located in Madurai, Tamil Nadu. It was built more than 2000 years ago and has been mentioned often in Tamil Sangam literature. The current structure was built during 17 CE, with 4 entrances & 10 Gopurams or towers – the largest tower measures over 50 meters in height. A thousand pillared hall, musical pillars, the Senthamarai Kulam (pond) and a sculpture museum can also be found inside the premises.

*Photo credit: Bernard Gagnon (Own work)
(http://commons.wikimedia.org/wiki/User:Bgag) [GFDL
(http://www.gnu.org/copyleft/fdl.html) or CC-BY-SA-3.0-2.5-2.0-1.0
(http://creativecommons.org/licenses/by-sa/3.0)], via Wikimedia Commons.*

2. Airavatesvara Temple, Tamil Nadu

The Airavatesvara Temple is in Darasuram, Tamil Nadu and was built by Raja Raja Chola II in 12 CE. One of the three great standing Chola temples, it is considered to be architecturally finer than the other two even though it's smaller. The Vimana is 24 m (80 feet) in height and the Mandapam is in the form of a huge stone chariot with stone wheels, drawn by horses. The pedestal of the balipeta has finely carved steps that produce music when someone strikes them.

Photo credit: Shriram Swaminathan (Own work) (http://commons.wikimedia.org/wiki/User:Shriram_Swaminathan) [CC-BY-SA-3.0 (http://creativecommons.org/licenses/by-sa/3.0)], via Wikimedia Commons.

3. Gangai-Konda-Cholapuram, Tamil Nadu

Did you know that the shadow of the 55m tall main tower of this temple never falls on the ground? The Gangai Konda Cholisvara temple was built by the Chola King Rajendra Chola I during 11 CE. Shortly afterwords, the Cholas (a dynasty with a South Indian empire) moved their capital from Thanjavur, and ruled South India for 250 years from there. An underground tunnel that connects the temple and palace has also been discovered. Everything except the temple is in ruins now. No one knows why this (erstwhile) capital was abandoned.

Photo credit: Kasiarunachalam at en.wikipedia
(http://en.wikipedia.org/wiki/User:Kasiarunachalam) [CC-BY-SA-3.0
(http://creativecommons.org/licenses/by-sa/3.0) or GFDL
(http://www.gnu.org/copyleft/fdl.html)], via Wikimedia Commons.

4. Brihadeeswarar Temple, Tamil Nadu

The Brihadeeswarar Temple is located in Thanjavur, Tamil Nadu. Constructed in the early 11th Century, it is one of the UNESCO World Heritage "Great Living Chola Temples". The temple tower/Vimana is 66 meters high and the Kalasha (topmost part) was built using a single 80 tonne stone. It was taken up using an inclined slope that started from 3 miles away! The entire Temple was built using 1,80,000 tonnes of granite, under orders of the famous Chola emperor Rajaraja Chola I.

Photo credit: Alagu (Flickr: Thanjavur Big Temple) (http://www.flickr.com/people/93904837@N00) [CC-BY-SA-2.0 (http://creativecommons.org/licenses/by-sa/2.0)], via Wikimedia Commons.

5. Pancha Rathas, Tamil Nadu

The Pancha Rathas in Mahabalipuram near Chennai are a group of UNESCO World Heritage monuments built by the Pallavas in 7-8 CE. There are five major monuments (rathas) that represents each Pandava brother in Mahabharatha (a great Indian Epic). These rock-cut sculptures were made by cutting a single large granite rock. It is estimated that even with many trained sculptors, these monuments would have taken a few years to complete! Each one is experimental and different.

Photo Credit: Nataraja (Own work)
(https://commons.wikimedia.org/wiki/User:Nataraja~commonswiki) [CC-BY-SA-2.5 (http://creativecommons.org/licenses/by-sa/2.5/deed.en)], via Wikimedia Commons.

6. Shore Temple, Tamil Nadu

The Shore Temple, also in Mahabalipuram, is the only surviving monument among seven similar ones that were constructed on the coast by the Pallavas in 7th Century CE. These temples were also used to guide ships, as the copper plates on their tops would reflect sunlight.

Photo credit: This photo was taken by me.

7. Kai-la-sa-nadhar Temple, Tamil Nadu

Kanchipuram is home to many old temples and was one of the five main pilgrimage centers of ancient India. The Kai-la-sa-nadhar temple here is one of the oldest structural temples in India. It was built during the 7th Century by Pallava Kings, and amazingly, still survives in its original shape. This is an ASI protected monument.

Photo credit: This photo was taken by me.

8. Silent Valley National Park, Kerala

Did you know that the biodiversity index of Silent Valley National Park is higher than that of the Amazon forests? Also known as Sairindhri Vanam, it is surrounded fully by Nilgiri Hills and located in the Palakkad District. Kunti river, flowing through this park, is famous for its crystal-clear water. A huge, hollow kathialying tree is located here – it can fit 12 people inside! Among other species, it is home to the Lion-tailed Macaque, Hairy-winged bat, Malabar giant squirrel, Flying squirrel, etc.

Photo credit: **നിരക്ഷരൻ** *at ml.wikipedia*
(http://commons.wikimedia.org/wiki/File%3ABhavani_puzha_-_silent_valley.jpg) [CC-BY-3.0 (http://creativecommons.org/licenses/by/3.0)], via Wikimedia Commons.

9. Mattancherry Palace & Paradesi Synagogue, Kerala

The Mattancherry Palace & Paradesi Synagogue in Kochi, Kerala, was built in 1555 by the Portuguese and renovated by the Dutch a century later. It is a unique combination of traditional Keralite & European architecture, and is famous for its wooden carvings & 16th Century paintings. In the nearby Jew town, there is an old (and functioning) synagogue constructed in 1568, and an 18th Century clock tower. Many Jews settled here during the medieval times.

Photo credit: Wouter Hagens (Own work)
(http://commons.wikimedia.org/wiki/User:Wouterhagens) [Public domain],
via Wikimedia Commons.

10. Vittala Temple, Karnataka

The Vittala Temple in Hampi, Karnataka, is the perfect example of the grandiose Vijayanagara art. Located at the center of the capital city of the erstwhile Vijayanagara empire, this temple houses impressive sculptures. The stone chariot is the symbol of Karnataka Tourism and the musical pillars make sounds when tapped on them (though visitors are restricted from doing that now). This majestic temple was destroyed after a war (along with the city) and stands half-burnt.

Photo credit: kanchan joshi (Own work) (https://commons.wikimedia.org/w/index.php?title=User:Joshi.k) [CC-BY-SA-3.0 (http://creativecommons.org/licenses/by-sa/3.0)], via Wikimedia Commons.

11. Pattadakal, Karnataka

Pattadakal in Karnataka, South India is a UNESCO World Heritage site that contains a number of ancient monuments built during 7 – 9 Century CE. Ten important temples built using both Dravidian (South Indian) and Nagara (North Indian) architectural styles – including a Jain temple – survive here today. These temples were built by the Kings of the Chalukya dynasty. The Sangameshvara temple is the oldest and Virupaksha temple is the largest. 7th Century CE inscriptions in both Kannada and Sanskrit have been found on this site.

Photo credit: Nithin bolar k (Own work)
(https://commons.wikimedia.org/w/index.php?title=User:Nithin_bolar_k)
[CC-BY-SA-3.0 (http://creativecommons.org/licenses/by-sa/3.0)], via
Wikimedia Commons.

12. Shravanabelagola, Karnataka

Shravanabelagola, located in Hassan District, Karnataka, is an important Jain pilgrimage center. The 57-feet tall statue of Gomateshwara Bahubali is considered to be one of the largest monolithic statues of its kind. Inscriptions near the statue date it to 981 CE. Chandragupta Maurya is said to have meditated and lived here during his last days, and Emperor Asoka constructed a monument dedicated to him on this site. There are two hills – Chandragiri & Vindhyagiri – nearby.

Photo credit: Sughoshdivanji (Own work)
(https://commons.wikimedia.org/w/index.php?title=User:Sughoshdivanji)
[CC-BY-SA-3.0 (http://creativecommons.org/licenses/by-sa/3.0)], via
Wikimedia Commons.

13. Churches of Old Goa, Goa

Old Goa, a city constructed initially in the 15th Century and the capital of Portuguese India until the 18th Century, was abandoned due to plague. There are many old churches & convents located in this area. One of them is the 400-year old Basillica of Bom Jesus (shown above) and it contains the body of St. Francis Xavier. This church is India's first minor Basilica and is a good example of Baroque architecture.

Photo credit: Samuel Abinezer (Own work) (https://commons.wikimedia.org/w/index.php?title=User:Samrockz29) [CC-BY-SA-3.0 (http://creativecommons.org/licenses/by-sa/3.0)], via Wikimedia Commons.

14. Golkonda Fort, Telangana

The Golkonda Fort in Hyderabad, Telangana, is situated on a 300 foot granite hill and was initially constructed in 10th Century CE. It was reconstructed in its present form by the King Ibrahim of the Qutub Shahi dynasty. The acoustic system was designed in a way that a clap on the bottom of the hill would be audible on the top of it (over 1 KM away). Golkonda is also famous for its diamond mines – the famous Koh-i-noor, Darya-i-noor & Hope diamonds were all excavated here.

Photo credit: Manish Maryada (Own work) (https://commons.wikimedia.org/w/index.php?title=User:Mrydrohit) [CC-BY-SA-3.0 (http://creativecommons.org/licenses/by-sa/3.0)], via Wikimedia Commons.

15. Qutb Shahi Tombs, Telangana

Qutb Shahi Tombs in Hyderabad, Telangana, were built in the 16th & 17th Century. These Tombs contain the remnants of most Qutb Shahi rulers. Neglected after the Qutb Shahi period, they were restored by Salar Jung III, during 19th Century. Mostly one or two storeyed buildings with a dome on the top, many tombs have masjids adjacent to them. Inscriptions have been found in Naskh, Tulth & Persian scripts. This site is close to the Golkonda Fort near Hyderabad.

Photo credit: Vamsi Varma (Own work) (https://commons.wikimedia.org/w/index.php?title=User:Vamsivarma7) [CC-BY-SA-3.0 (http://creativecommons.org/licenses/by-sa/3.0)], via Wikimedia Commons.

West & Central India

1. Gwalior Fort, Madhya Pradesh

Gwalior Fort in Gwalior, Madhya Pradesh, is one of the largest forts of India. It was built during the 8th Century CE and is spread over 3 Sq. km. The fort wall is 11m in height; this fort has been at the center of important historical events, including the Rani of Jhansi battle against the British. There are many important structures inside this palace like the Man Mandir Palace, Gujari Mahal, Jehangir Mahal, Karan Palace, Shahjahan Mahal, etc. The water reservoir holds sufficient water for 15,000 people.

Photo credit: Aniisng7 (Own work) (https://commons.wikimedia.org/w/index.php?title=User:Aniisng7) [CC-BY-SA-3.0 (http://creativecommons.org/licenses/by-sa/3.0)], via Wikimedia Commons.

2. Khajuraho, Madhya Pradesh

The Khajuraho group of monuments/temples is located in Madhya Pradesh. Built by Chandela Rajputs between 950 & 1150 CE, Khajuraho contains a group of Hindu & Jain Temples, and is popular for its architecture and erotic sculptures. There were originally 85 temples, but only 25 stand today. These temples were made using sandstone (without mortar) and are held together by gravity.

Photo credit: Aryan Akwarya (Own work) (https://commons.wikimedia.org/w/index.php?title=User:Aryan_Akwarya) [CC-BY-SA-3.0 (http://creativecommons.org/licenses/by-sa/3.0)], via Wikimedia Commons.

3. Mandu Group of Monuments, Madhya Pradesh

The Mandu/Mandavgad is a group of monuments that are the remnants of a ruined city. It was a fortified city even in 6th Century BCE, and was the capital of many kingdoms and dynasties. Mandu contains both natural and man-made fortifications (incl. a 37 km wall and 12 gates) all along the outer boundary. Many palaces, temples, mosques and other monuments, built as early as 14th Century CE, have survived.

Photo credit: Lukas Vacovsky (Own work) (https://commons.wikimedia.org/w/index.php?title=User:Lukas_vacovsky) [CC-BY-SA-3.0 (http://creativecommons.org/licenses/by-sa/3.0)], via Wikimedia Commons.

4. Orchha, Madhya Pradesh

Founded in 15th Century CE by Bundela chief Rudrapratap Singh, Orchha is situated along the Betwa river near Jhansi. It is an abandoned city that resembles a ghost town, and has numerous palaces, temples, tombs, and residential complexes of a bygone era, most of which are in ruins. Notable buildings – they combine Rajput & Mughal architectures – include the Jehangir Mahal, Raja Mahal, Chaturbuj Temple, Lakshmi Temple, Ram Raja Temple, and Chhatris along the bank of Betwa river.

Photo credit: YashiWong (Own work) (https://commons.wikimedia.org/w/index.php?title=User:YashiWong) [GFDL (http://www.gnu.org/copyleft/fdl.html) or CC-BY-SA-3.0-2.5-2.0-1.0 (http://creativecommons.org/licenses/by-sa/3.0)], via Wikimedia Commons.

5. Sanchi Stupa, Madhya Pradesh

The Sanchi Stupa in Madhya Pradesh, is a UNESCO World Heritage monument. It consists of various ancient Buddhist monuments built in 3 BCE - 12 CE. The 'Great Stupa' is the oldest surviving monument in India and was built by Emperor Asoka of the Mauryan dynasty during 3rd Century BCE. The multi-tiered dome is a symbol of Dharma – the wheel of the law. A new University of Buddhist and Indic studies will be coming up near this location shortly.

Photo credit: Abhinav Varshney (Own work)
(https://commons.wikimedia.org/w/index.php?title=User:Abhinav_Varshney)
[CC-BY-SA-3.0 (http://creativecommons.org/licenses/by-sa/3.0)], via
Wikimedia Commons.

6. Chhtrapati Shivaji Terminus, Maharashtra

The Chhtrapati Shivaji Terminus (CST) in Mumbai, is a UNESCO World Heritage monument. Designed by Frederick William Stevens and built in 1888 CE in the High Victorian Italianate Gothic revival architecture style – along with elements of Indian architecture – this was previously called Victoria Terminus (VT). It houses the headquarters of Central Indian Railways and has 18 railway platforms (11 long-distance & 7 local). Notice the statue above the topmost dome?

Photo credit: Dbenbenn (Own work)
(https://de.wikipedia.org/wiki/User:Sebastianjude) [CC-BY-SA-3.0
(http://creativecommons.org/licenses/by-sa/3.0)], via Wikimedia Commons.

7. Elephanta Caves, Maharashtra

The Elephanta Caves near Mumbai, located on an island called Gharapuri or Dharapuri, have been designated a UNESCO World Heritage site. This site contains rock-cut cave temples with huge pillars and sculptures, estimated to have been built during 4 – 6 Century CE. The idols (some of them over 5m tall) and carvings represent mythological events both in Hindu and Buddhist religions. You have to board a ferry from Gateway of India, Mumbai, to reach this picturesque and historic island.

Picture credit: Philip Larson (originally posted to Flickr as DSC04527) (http://flickr.com/photos/22098403@N00) [CC-BY-SA-2.0 (http://creativecommons.org/licenses/by-sa/2.0)], via Wikimedia Commons.

8. Ajanta Caves, Maharashtra

The Ajanta Caves in Aurangabad district, Maharashtra, are rock-cut caves constructed at various periods in between 2nd Century BCE and 6th Century CE. They were used as a place of teaching by Buddhist monks. The caves are very popular for their exotic setting, extensive paintings & brilliant sculptures. Lost to the world until 19th Century CE (after they were abandoned), these caves were rediscovered by a British officer.

Photo credit: Danial Chitnis (originally posted to Flickr as Ajanta Caves) (http://flickr.com/photos/83407683@N00) [CC-BY-2.0 (http://creativecommons.org/licenses/by/2.0)], via Wikimedia Commons.

9. Ellora Caves, Maharashtra

Ellora Caves Near the Ajanta caves, are a group of rock-cut monuments consisting of 34 cave structures excavated out of the vertical face of Charanandri hills. They were built by Rashtrakutas mostly between 5 – 10th Century CE. There are living quarters, sleeping quarters, rooms, kitchens, and Hindu, Buddhist and Jain Temples within these multi-story carved monuments. Many sculptures here were sculpted to resemble shapes made of wood.

Photo credit: Soumitra Inamdar (Own work) (https://commons.wikimedia.org/w/index.php?title=User:Soumitra911) [CC-

BY-SA-3.0 (http://creativecommons.org/licenses/by-sa/3.0)], via Wikimedia Commons.

10. Gir Forest & National Park, Gujarat

The Gir National Park was established in 1965 covering 1412 sq. km, including the forest. In spite of early conservation efforts, the count of Asiatic Lions were reduced to a mere 15 due to heavy hunting during early 20th Century. In 2010, their count had increased to 411. There are many species of animals, birds and plants in the forest. There are 7 perennial rivers & 4 dams that provide water in this desert area. A Gir Interpretation Zone within the sanctuary is open to visitors.

Photo credit: Mayankvagadiya (Own work)
(https://commons.wikimedia.org/w/index.php?title=User:Mayankvagadiya)
[CC-BY-SA-3.0 (http://creativecommons.org/licenses/by-sa/3.0)], via
Wikimedia Commons.

11. Champaner-Pavagadh, Gujarat

Champaner, a medieval city built during 16th Century CE by Mahmud Begada, was abandoned soon after creation and has been so ever since. It has well preserved medieval urban fabric including sandstone-carved mosques and tombs. The neighboring Pavagadh hills have recorded history from 2nd Century BCE and contains, among others, an ancient fort as well as Hindu and Jain temples. It is a popular pilgrimage center even today.

Photo credit: Anupamg (Own work)
(http://commons.wikimedia.org/wiki/User:Anupamg) [CC-BY-SA-3.0
(http://creativecommons.org/licenses/by-sa/3.0)], via Wikimedia Commons.

12. Rani ki vav, Gujarat

Rani Ki Vav in Patan, Gujarat, is a large step-well to fetch water. Built in 1063 CE by Queen Udayamati in memory of King Bhimdev I, this step-well measures 64m(l)x20m(w)x27m(d). Flooded by the Saraswati river and silted-over until the late 1980s, this site retains more than 800 intricately carved sculptures, among seven galleries. Other features include pillared multi-storyed pavilions at regular intervals and a 30 Km long tunnel below the last step.

Photo credit: Azaz.sayyad (Own work) (https://commons.wikimedia.org/w/index.php?title=User:Azaz.sayyad) [CC-

BY-SA-3.0 (http://creativecommons.org/licenses/by-sa/3.0)], via Wikimedia Commons.

13. Somnath Temple, Gujarat

The Somnath Temple in Gujarat has been one of the most destroyed and re-constructed temples in India. Somnath Temple stands on the shore of Arabian Sea on the Western coast of India. It is one of the oldest temples in the country, and has been mentioned in many ancient texts. It is believed that Lord Krishna, an incarnation of Lord Vishnu – one of the main deities of Indian mythology – took his last journey to the abodes of heaven from here. The temple is for Lord Shiva, and is one of the 12 main holy Jyotrlinga sites in India. There is an arrow that indicates the unobstructed sea route from this temple to the South Pole, which is 9936 K.M away!

Photo credit: BeautifulEyes (Own work) (https://commons.wikimedia.org/w/index.php?title=User:BeautifulEyes) [CC-BY-SA-3.0 (http://creativecommons.org/licenses/by-sa/3.0)], via Wikimedia Commons.

East India

1. Bhitarkanika National Park, Odisha

Spread over an area of 672 sq. km, Bhitarkanika National Park is the second largest Mangrove forest and wetland ecosystem in India. It is surrounded by the Bhitarkanika wildlife sanctuary and is famous for Olive Ridley sea-turtles, white crocodiles, pythons, cobras, and water monitor lizards, among others. Salt water crocodiles here can grow up to 6 meters in length! There are also more than 215 species of birds and many migratory ones, including eight varieties of the kingfisher, darters, and black ibis.

Photo credit: Jayanth Sharma
(https://en.wikipedia.org/wiki/User:Jayanthsharma) [CC-BY-3.0 (http://creativecommons.org/licenses/by/3.0)], via Wikimedia Commons.

2. Konark Sun Temple, Odisha

The Konark Sun Temple is a UNESCO World Heritage Monument and was built around 1250 CE by Narasimhadeva I. The structure was built to resemble a giant chariot with wheels and horses, but a large portion of it is in ruins now. This photo shows the surviving 30m high structure. In fact, there was a larger, temple-like structure (70m tall), right in front of it earlier. This site is famous for its brilliantly carved intricate sculptures.

Picture credit: Chaitali Chowdhury (Own work) (https://commons.wikimedia.org/w/index.php?title=User:Photolover) [CC-BY-SA-3.0 (http://creativecommons.org/licenses/by-sa/3.0)], via Wikimedia Commons.

3. Mahabodhi Temple, Bihar

The Mababodhi Temple complex in Bodh Gaya (initially called Uruwela) is near Patna in Bihar. It is the place where Gautama Buddha is considered to have attained enlightenment. Constructed by Emperor Asoka, the temple was renovated in the 1st Century CE. This 55m tall structure can be seen from 11 KM away, but it was rediscovered only in the 19th Century, after being abandoned centuries earlier. The holy Bodhi tree here is a sapling of the original Bodhi tree.

Photo credit: Ken Weiland
(http://www.flickr.com/photos/wieland7/3639641115/)
(http://www.flickr.com/photos/wieland7/3639641115/) [CC-BY-SA-2.0

(http://creativecommons.org/licenses/by-sa/2.0)], via Wikimedia Commons.

4. Sher Shah Suri Tomb, Bihar

The Sher Shah Suri Tomb in Sasaram, Bihar, is a UNESCO World Heritage monument built by Sher Shah Suri himself, and completed by his son Islam Shah in 1545 CE. The octagonal tomb is made of red sandstone and is situated at the center of a man-made square lake. From being the son of a normal jagirdar, Sher Shah Suri went on to defeat the Mughal Empire (King Humayun) and ruled India for 5 years. His administrative, building, and revenue collection methods helped Mughal Emperor Akbar create a strong central structure later on.

Photo credit: Nandanupadhyay (Own work)
(http://commons.wikimedia.org/wiki/User:Nandanupadhyay) [CC-BY-SA-3.0
(http://creativecommons.org/licenses/by-sa/3.0)], via Wikimedia Commons.

5. Neora Valley National Park, West Bengal

Situated in the Darjeeling district (that is also home to the famous hill-station) and spread over 88 sq. km, this is one of the richest biological zones in North-East India. Famous for the Red Panda and having natural forests, hills, lakes, orchids & bamboo trees, much of Neora Valley National park is unexplored. The highest point of the park is located at an elevation of 10,600 feet and the Neora river runs through it.

Photo credit: Anirban Biswas (Flickr)
(http://flickr.com/photos/25966716@N00) [CC-BY-SA-2.0
(http://creativecommons.org/licenses/by-sa/2.0)], via Wikimedia Commons.

6. Shantiniketan, West Bengal

Based on the philosophy that learning in a natural environment can be more enjoyable & fruitful, Rabindranath Tagore built the famous Visva-Bharti University in Shantiniketan, using money obtained from his Nobel Prize for Literature. Shantiniketan consists of various institutions including Kala Bhavana, Art College; Sangit Bhavana, Institute of Music; and Vinaya Bhavana, Institute of Education. Among other events, the 3-day Poush Mela – held in the last week of December – is very popular.

Photo credit: This is a copyright free image released in the public domain.

7. Sundarbans National Park, West Bengal

The Sundarbans National Park is a UNESCO World Heritage site along with Sundarbans, Bangladesh. It's a huge biosphere reserve with dense mangrove forests and complex intersection of water channels that include 7 major rivers. The eco-geography of this area is dependent on two flow/ebb tides that occurs within 24 hours, covering most of the region. The only way to get around the Sundarbans is by boat. This place is home to many rare species of flora & fauna and is also the largest reserve for Bengal tigers.

Photo credit: bri vos (Flickr) (http://flickr.com/photos/78392587@N00)

[CC-BY-2.0 (http://creativecommons.org/licenses/by/2.0)], via Wikimedia Commons.

8. Bishnupur Temples, West Bengal

The Bishnupur Temples in Bankur District, West Bengal, are a group of temples built by Malla rulers from 17th Century CE. These temples are unique in their architectural style and were built using clay-bricks and terracota tiles, made from laterite stones. All the temples used curved roofs instead of straight ones, and have extensive engravings, terracota sculptures on walls and reliefs. They mostly portray scenes from Ramayana & Mahabharata [the Hindu epics]. This photo shows the Shyam-Raya Temple (Panch Chura) that is dedicated to Lord Krishna.

Photo credit: Amartyabag (Own work) (https://commons.wikimedia.org/w/index.php?title=User:Amartyabag) [CC-BY-SA-3.0 (http://creativecommons.org/licenses/by-sa/3.0)], via Wikimedia Commons.

9. Victoria Memorial, West Bengal

Victoria Memorial is a very prominent landmark in Kolkata, West Bengal. Inaugurated in 1921, this complex has been converted into a museum that houses rare artifacts of the British India period. The building (including the dome) is 56 meters tall and has 64 acres of gardens surrounding it.

Photo credit: Vipin8169 (Own work) (https://commons.wikimedia.org/w/index.php?title=User:Vipin8169) [CC-BY-SA-3.0 (http://creativecommons.org/licenses/by-sa/3.0)], via Wikimedia Commons.

10. Kaziranga National Park, Assam

The Kaziranga National Park in Assam is the perfect place for you to go to if you love jungles. Declared a World Heritage Site, Kaziranga is home to a number of rare fauna including the One-Horned Rhinoceroses, wild boars, wild water buffaloes, tigers, the Great Indian Hornbill, the Indian Roller, brown tortoises, and so on. With the Bhramaputra river criss-crossing the site and a number of other water bodies and lush green forests, what more could a nature-lover ask for?

Photo credit: Dcmpuri (Own work) (https://commons.wikimedia.org/w/index.php?title=User:Dcmpuri) [CC-BY-SA-3.0 (http://creativecommons.org/licenses/by-sa/3.0)], via Wikimedia Commons.

11. Majuli River Island, Assam

The Majuli River Island in Assam is the largest riverine island in the world. Situated within the braided Brahmaputra river (that stretches up to 10 miles at its widest point!), the island was a part of the mainland until it was separated by an earthquake and newly created river channels during the 18th Century. Majuli has a population of more than 1,50,000 people living in 144 villages. Initially, the island covered an area of 1250 sq. km, but due to erosion, only 421 sq. km remains. It is famous for its handlooms and varieties of rice & pottery.

Photo credit: Kalai Sukanta from Shillong, India (Majuli Island,Assam) (http://www.flickr.com/people/52142724@N02) [CC-BY-2.0 (http://creativecommons.org/licenses/by/2.0) or CC-BY-2.0 (http://creativecommons.org/licenses/by/2.0)], via Wikimedia Commons.

12. Manas National Park, Assam

Manas National Park in Assam is located on the foothills of the Eastern Himalayas and covers 950 Sq. km. It is contiguous with the Royal Manas National Park, Bhutan and the Manas river flows through it. Many rare animals like the Indian Rhinoceros, Asian Water Buffaloes, Capped Langur and so on can be found here. Others like Pygmy Hot, Assam Roofed Turtle & Golden Langur are found only in this park. More than 450 species of birds and 543 species of vegetation have been identified. Nature trails, jungle safari, river rafting are popular activities for travelers.

Picture credit: daimalu (http://flickr.com/photos/18456139@N00) [CC-BY-2.0 (http://creativecommons.org/licenses/by/2.0)], via Wikimedia Commons.

13. Namdapha National Park, Arunachal Pradesh

Namdapha National Park in Arunachal Pradesh is located in the Eastern Himalayas. It is the third largest natural park in India, covering 1985 sq. km. It encompasses a large evergreen forest with an abundance of bamboo trees. Many rare species like Red Panda, Himalayan Wood-owl, and Blue Venda (endangered orchid), can be found here. Namdapha is also a tiger reserve and the only place in the world that contains tigers as well as three leopard species (incl. snow leopard and clouded leopard). This is also the only park in india where apes can be seen.

Photo credit: Aparajita Datta (Own work)
(https://commons.wikimedia.org/w/index.php?title=User:Aparajita_Datta)
[CC-BY-SA-3.0 (http://creativecommons.org/licenses/by-sa/3.0)], via
Wikimedia Commons.

14. Khangchendronga National Park, Sikkim

Khangchendronga National Park, also known as Kanchanjunga, is in Sikkim. This 850 sq. km protected high-altitude national park is located along the Kanchanjunga peak, the third highest mountain in the world; it contains many glaciers in its range. Trekking is a popular activity here especially in the months of April and May, although a permit is required to enter this region. The park is popular for rare animals like snow leapord, red panda, Himalayan tahr, musk deer, etc.

Picture credit: Tony Hisgett from Birmingham, UK (Red Panda Uploaded by tm) (http://www.flickr.com/people/37804979@N00) [CC-BY-2.0 (http://creativecommons.org/licenses/by/2.0)], via Wikimedia Commons.

India: 50 Must Do Things

1. See a Bollywood/Regional Language Movie

If you want to understand the Indian way of life little bit and have a lot of fun at the same time, watch a Bollywood and/or regional language movie in a cinema hall, wherever you stay.

Theaters might not show sub-titles in English, but don't be bothered about it – go ahead and watch it anyway. Better still, watch movies in multiple Indian languages on the same day. You'll be able to follow the story even though you may not understand the dialogues.

Indian movies are colorful and energetic. Even though the situations portrayed can be exaggerated, they still offer a 'culture-lens' with which you can understand India.

Most movies are also emotional affairs so be ready to experience a culture shock! Indian movies are quite long (on an average, 2-2.5 hours) and (try to) pack all emotions like joy, sorrow, humor, music (songs), dance, etc. Tip: Don't try to analyze the story or find any logic in the scenes presented. Just enjoy :)

Watching Indian movies is a lot of fun, especially for people viewing them for the first time. Before you go, though, do find out which movies are doing well in the box-office. If a movie is running for more than 50 days or some big stars are acting in them, it should be good.

However, if you want to watch only excellent movies, I will give you the names of some movies that I loved watching over the years -

#S.No. Movie - Language

#1. Chak de India – Hindi
#2. Anjali – Tamil
#3. Lagaan – Hindi
#4. Padayappa – Tamil
#5. Vicky Donor – Hindi
#6. English Vinglish – Hindi
#7. Roja – Tamil/Hindi
#8. Mouna Raagam – Tamil
#9. Dilwale Dulhaniyan Le Jaayenge (DDLJ) – Hindi
#10. Sholay – Hindi
#11. Indian – Tamil
#12. Aankhen – Hindi
#13. Gilli – Tamil
#14. 3 Idiots - Hindi
#15. Jaane Tu Ya Jaane Naa - Hindi

*** Movies from Hindi and Tamil have been suggested because I am familiar with movies in these two languages. There are many more excellent movies in multiple languages of India – just ask people around you.

You can buy the DVDs for these movies (or any other movie) from Flipkart.com and Amazon.in, after you reach India. DVDs generally come with English sub-titles. However, do check before buying.

Photo Credit: ClickInfraSolutions (Own work) (https://commons.wikimedia.org/w/index.php?title=User:Clickinfrasolutions) [CC-BY-SA-4.0 (https://commons.wikimedia.org/wiki/Category:CC-BY-SA-4.0)], via Wikimedia Commons.

2. Eat Indian Sweets & Savories

India is a country with a sweet tooth. Indian sweets can be overly sweet but have great flavor. They differ from culture to culture and region to region. As with all sweet foods, moderation is the key to their enjoyment and good-health.

Where do I even start with my favorites? Gulab Jamun, Rasagulla, Rasamilai, Jilebi, Laddu, Halwa, Milk Peda, Cashew (based) sweets, Badam or almond (based) sweets, the list goes on.

Usually, there are separate shops selling sweets and savories, like pastry shops of the West. You can go into any one of them and try out different varieties. Do remember — every locality has its specialty sweets. Find out from the shopkeeper and taste them too.

Savories are crispy Indian snacks, like chips. There are a

large number of savories that you will find in sweet and other shops across India. With chips, try eating potato chips, finger chips, banana chips, etc. The most common savory is Mixer - a mix of different savories that comes in various combinations. There are many more local savories, depending on the region you visit.

You can either buy sweets/savories in packets or according to your requirement (by their weight - 100g, 250g, 500g, etc). In South and West India, savories are also eaten as a side dish with main course dishes like rice or chapati (bread).

Photo Credit: Manish Ricku (Own work) (https://commons.wikimedia.org/w/index.php?title=User:Manish_Ricku)[CC-BY-SA-4.0 (https://commons.wikimedia.org/wiki/Category:CC-BY-SA-4.0)], via Wikimedia Commons.

3. Listen to Indian (Popular) Music

Many Indian movies include songs. These songs are mostly shot in exotic sets/locations, and some of them may even feature multiple dancers. Of course, it's often artificial reality but a lot of fun to watch, nevertheless. Indian movie songs are colorful, and take inspiration from cultures around the world.

You can flip through TV channels until you find one that is dedicated to playing Indian movie songs. Better still, tune into any Indian FM radio station (from your cell phone/MP3 player) and listen to the songs presented there. Generally, radio channels play the latest hit film songs.

You can visit music streaming websites or music streaming apps and listen to new and popular songs. Youtube also has a great collection - you can see/listen to movie songs from anywhere.

Some of my all-time favorite movie songs are given below,

#Sno. Song – Movie (Language)

#1. Chinna Chinna Aasai – Roja (Tamil)
#2. Sheila ki jawani – Tees Maar Khan (Hindi)
#3. Chayya Chayya – Dil Se (Hindi)
#4. Oorvasi oorvasi – Kadhalan (Tamil)
#5. Aamani Padave koyila – Geethanjali (Telugu)
#6. Anagasire yaako indhu – Mungaru Male (Kannada)
#7. Vaseegara – Minnale (Tamil)
#8. Chaanjadi Aadi – Adaminte Maakan Abu (Malayalam)
#9. Luv ka the end – Luv ka the end (Hindi)
#10. Pyar mein – Thank you (Hindi)
#11. Mera man – Tell me O'Kkhuda (Hindi)
#12. Why this kolaveri di – 3 (Tamil)
#13. Character deela – Ready (Hindi)
#14. Ek ladki ko dekha to – 1942 A Love Story (Hindi)
#15. Tanha tanha – Rangeela (Hindi)

Photo Credit: Vivek. k. Verma (Own work) (https://commons.wikimedia.org/w/index.php?title=User:Vivek.k.Verma) [CC-BY-SA-4.0 (https://commons.wikimedia.org/wiki/Category:CC-BY-SA-4.0)], via Wikimedia Commons.

4. Drink Indian Tea

A tea is a tea is a tea, right? Wrong! Indian tea is unique since it is made by mixing liberal quantities of milk and sugar (along with fresh tea-powder). In India, the beverage is sweet and tasty! Some places might even serve you masala tea, green tea, lime tea, and other varieties. There are some popular local brands like Darjeeling Tea. When in India, you can walk into any Indian restaurant and order for a chai, as its called here.

Tea tastes better if you eat something along with it. Buy a packet of Brittania milk biscuits or Marie biscuits (any nearby shop will have these), dip the biscuits into the tea, eat them, and then drink the tea. Pure bliss, I tell you!

Combining tea with something spicy works even better. If you are in South India, ask for medhu vada/masal vada/sambar vada/bajji (in any restaurant). There are various snacks across India, just ask around to find out what they can serve you with the hot tea. It will be worth it.

Photo Credit: Bharath P.S (Own work) (https://commons.wikimedia.org/w/index.php?title=User:Psbharath619) [CC-BY-SA-4.0 (https://commons.wikimedia.org/wiki/Category:CC-BY-SA-4.0)], via Wikimedia Commons.

5. Eat Chat Items

This is not 'chat' as in web-chat. It's pronounced more like 'Chaat' and is a hugely popular Indian snack. Chat items are spicy (and hot), but extremely tasty. Yes, you need to be a brave-heart to eat some of these things, especially if you are not used to spicy cuisine. The enjoyment is unlimited, though :D

I'll suggest some less-spicy items first: Try eating pav-bhaji - it's basically puffed bread/bun (pav) and comes with vegetable masala (bhaji). The combination (along with lime & onion) tastes nice. You can add less bhaji to each piece of the bread, if you find it too spicy. Dahi (curd/yogurt) based chat items are relatively less spicy too, but not any less tasty! Try dahi-puri, dahi-papdi or any other dahi-based chat item available.

When you are ready to go to the next level, you can eat bhel-puri. It's somewhat spicy, but one of my favorites. You can also try samosa, kachori, bread-channa, samosa-channa, etc. These items are considerably spicier.

If you want to try something really spicy and zingy, eat pani-puri/golgappa, which is available in slightly different forms across India. They fill sweet and spicy liquids into a small puri (along with some masala) and give it to you one by one. You need to eat each pani-puri in a single gulp. Generally, a plate consists of 6-8 pani-puris.

Mostly shops selling sweets/savories as well as some restaurants sell chat items. But there are many smaller street shops that sell these items exclusively. Stick with the larger shops/restaurants as far as possible.

Photo Credit: Rupamdas75 (Own work)
(https://commons.wikimedia.org/w/index.php?title=User:Rupamdas75) [CC-BY-SA-4.0 (https://commons.wikimedia.org/wiki/Category:CC-BY-SA-4.0)], via Wikimedia Commons.

India: 55 Must See Places & 50 Must Do Things

6. Glance through a newspaper

While reading multiple articles in a newspaper is difficult, glancing through the newspaper here is actually a pleasure! The headlines will enable you to know the latest happenings, current affairs, and trending topics in the country. If you want to pick up a conversation with a local person, you can try talking about some topics mentioned in the day's newspaper. Avoid politics and religion as far as possible – they are sensitive issues. Talk instead about cricket, movies, music, business, tourist places to visit, what to eat, etc., and you will make instant friends.

Newspapers (mostly the supplements) will also provide information on movies, events, screenings, workshops, exhibitions, etc., happening in the city. While in India, glance through the sports-section and become slightly cricket-literate.

Some good newspapers in India are (in no particular

order): The Hindu, Times of India, Hindustan Times, Deccan Chronicle, DNA India, The Deccan Herald, and so on. If you are interested in current affairs, you can also buy magazines like India Today, The Week, Outlook, etc.

Photo Credit: Shajankumar (Own work) (https://commons.wikimedia.org/w/index.php?title=User:Shajankumar) [CC-BY-SA-3.0 (https://creativecommons.org/licenses/by-sa/3.0/deed.en)], via Wikimedia Commons.

7. Eat Indian breakfast

The breakfast menu, like all other food, differs from place to place. If you stay in large hotels, you'll get a Western breakfast. You can walk into any restaurant, glance through the menu card and choose from the multiple items mentioned there.

Some of the favorite breakfast items are:

Idly, Rava Idly (Mostly eaten with hands). Check if sambar idly, fried idly or kaima idly is available – you can eat these items with a spoon. You can also order vada/sambar vada, along with idly.

Dosa/Masala Dosa (Mostly eaten with hands) – You should eat at least one masala dosa before leaving India - it's too good!

The above two items come with sambar/chutney. Cut a

small piece of idly/dosa, dip it in sambar (liquid) or chutney (semi-solid) and then eat it.

You can also eat,
Upma/Khichidi, Poori, Pongal, Parota in South India.
Chapati, Roti, Naan, Parantha, Sabji (various types) in North India.
Bhajiya, vada, farsan in Western/Central India.

Most Indian breakfast items are eaten with the hands. The basic ingredient used in most breakfast items is rice or wheat.

Photo Credit: Ewan Munro (Own work) (http://www.flickr.com/people/55935853@N00) [CC-BY-SA-2.0 (https://creativecommons.org/licenses/by-sa/2.0/deed.en)], via Wikimedia Commons.

8. Travel in a Train

The best way to explore the brilliant sights of Indian landscapes is to travel in a train (window seat, preferably) from one town/city to another. You can also stand behind the open coach door and experience the sights along with the breeze. However, make sure you stand at a safe distance from the door. If you are interested in watching the scenery, also avoid night journeys and A/C compartments, as you will not be able to see much outside.

Not only the sights, but even the sounds made by a train while moving on the track, is very interesting. Train journeys in India are quite safe, but it is best not to buy anything from the local vendors who come to sell food-items on the train (they may not be hygienic). Also, basic rule, don't accept any food/beverage from strangers!

Train loos may not be maintained very well, but this is a

small (and often tolerable) inconvenience. Just go once (on a short journey) if you are a cleanliness freak. Trains in India can be very long, quite slow, and filled with people. So take care while planning your journey.

Also, check if there are any special super-luxury trains that run exclusively for tourists available in the region. Some great examples: Palace on Wheels, Deccan Odyssey, The Golden Chariot, and The Indian Maharaja. These trains are a good choice if you want to enjoy your travel in leisure and with superb hospitality.

You can book train tickets online; it is better to book them in advance (at least one month before the journey) to ensure that you get a seat. Unreserved compartments are available, but are overcrowded. So it is better to avoid them.

There are also electric trains available in certain cities (for local intra-city travel). Traveling in electric trains is a unique experience in India. You can travel in them during off-peak hours to start with and get a good idea. If there is a functioning Metro rail service in the city you visit, don't hesitate to use that too.

Photo Credit: Brhaspati (Own work)
(https://commons.wikimedia.org/wiki/User:Brhaspati) [CC-BY-SA-3.0 (https://creativecommons.org/licenses/by-sa/3.0/deed.en)], via Wikimedia Commons.

9. Eat Indian Fruits/Drink Fruit Juices

Of course, you get fruits and juices everywhere in the world. But, there maybe many fruits that are commonly available in India that may not be available in your part of the world. Go to shops selling fruits or super-markets, browse through the produce kept there and buy anything that you are not familiar with. All fruits are healthy - you know that. Ensure that you wash the fruits with water before eating them.

Some fruits that maybe uncommon in your place: Banana (yellow, green, red), Papaya, Sweet Lime (Musambi), Sapodilla (Suppota/Chickoo), Pomegranate, Mango, Jack fruit, Sugar apple/sweetsop (Seetha Pazham/Seetha phal), Water melon, Guava, and so on. A lot of dry-fruits like dates, raisins, etc. are also commonly available in India.

Juice shops have a variety of fruit juices and may offer a mix of two or more fruits in a single juice. These often have fancy names given to them. I suggest you drink at least one fruit juice per day - there is no better/healthier/tastier way to prevent dehydration on a hot or humid day in India!

Juices are normally prepared from fresh fruits, right in front of your eyes. If you are visiting a small shop, insist on mineral water to be used while making the juice. It's highly recommended that you buy and carry mineral water, too. Local water may not be suitable for drinking at many places (except in large hotels/restaurants, homes, etc).

Photo Credit: Joe Zachs (Own work)
(http://www.flickr.com/photos/joezach/54030635/) [CC-BY-SA-2.0 (https://creativecommons.org/licenses/by-sa/2.0/deed.en)], via Wikimedia Commons.

10. Wear traditional Indian clothes

What's the fun in visiting a place if you don't try the dress worn by the local people? India's clothing, like its food, is unique, varied and culture–based. A saree is an exotic (but common) dress in India. It's basically a long piece of cloth draped across the body. The way women wear it is an art (and tradition) that has been passed on over many centuries.

A saree also needs a matching blouse and inner garments. You can select these materials and get them stitched if you have time. Otherwise, just wrap the saree around T-shirt/jeans! You can ask the assistants (at the shop where you buy the saree) to teach you how to wear it - they'll be glad to help. Or you can view the videos available on "how to wear a saree" in Youtube. There are many different ways!

The chance that you'll see women in a heavy saree in major Indian cities is small, since many have adopted Western wear. But, if you go to a wedding, festivals, functions or visit a local Temple, you can see many women dressed in sarees. In small towns and rural areas, they are more common.

There is also the churidar/salwar that women wear. This is a relatively uncomplicated dress; you can buy a ready-made salwar-kameez/churidar-dupatta according to your size and wear it instantly. Kurtas are tops that can even be worn on Western pants and denims.

The best thing about Indian dresses is the variety and the vivid colors and designs. There are different types of materials available - from cotton to silk to Georgette. A good saree should be available for $10 - $100 (Rs. 500 – Rs. 5000, approx). If you want to buy an expensive saree, there is no upper limit to the pricing. Generally, silk sarees are the most expensive (and also the heaviest) but cotton sarees are cheaper and comfortable to wear.

Now to the men. If you want to sport a traditional look, buy a white silk shirt and silk dhoti (or cotton ones). But then, if you expect other Indian men to be wearing this dress, you'll mostly be disappointed (except if you visit villages). Many men wear kurtas with jeans or pants. There is much less variety for traditional daily wear for men, usually everyone sticks to pants and shirts. In traditional events and functions though, you will see heavy kurtas, turbans and bejewelled shoes.

Photo Credit: Sreekumar K.S (Own work) (http://flickr.com/photos/83588790@N00)[CC-BY-SA-2.0 (https://creativecommons.org/licenses/by-sa/2.0/deed.en)], via Wikimedia Commons.

11. Visit a place of worship

India is the land of a thousand Gods and a million temples. Hinduism is the major religion in India, but the country also has a considerable number of people belonging to Muslim, Christian, Sikh, Parsi, Jain, and other religions, and consequently there are a large number of places of worship that are often landmarks in themselves.

You can find various such in every city, town and village that you visit. The most interesting thing about a place of worship is often its architecture. These also contain a lot of artistic carvings and statues in stone, wood, etc. In short – they are a treat to the eyes.

Most of these places will allow foreigners inside, but some of them may not allow foreigners at certain parts of the complex. Avoid taking photographs inside unless it's allowed.

Don't miss eating the prasad/food-offering given in many places, which is generally quite tasty. You can buy various sweets and other offerings outside the complexes, especially near temples and gurudwaras.

There are many large, old and historically famous places of worship. You can check the history of your place of visit to find out more about these. Many popular temples and other places have big visiting crowds, so you'll probably spend a few hours standing in long queues!

Photo Credit: This photo was taken by me.

12. Eat the Biryani

If there is a single Indian dish that you should definitely eat before leaving India, it is the biryani. This dish is made of basmati rice (a long-grained, flavourful variety of rice) and various nuts and spices. Based on the restaurant offering it, you will get onion-raitha (onion mixed with curd) or you may have to order some other side-dish. You get vegetable biryani (vegan), chicken biriyani, mutton biryani, etc. The only downside to biryani is that it can be quite spicy!

If you want a less spicy version, try eating Pulav or fried rice. There are various varieties: vegetable pulav, peas pulav, kashmiri (dry-fruits) pulav, etc. All of them are excellent! The common side-dishes available include aloo mutter (potato-peas curry), aloo gobi (potato-cauliflower curry), paneer mutter masala (dry butter-peas curry), mixed vegetable kurma, etc. Since I am a vegetarian, I cannot tell you much about the non-vegetarian options. But there are many.

One side dish is (generally) sufficient for two people. You can eat the biryani/pulav & side-dish using two spoons, or one spoon and one fork.

If there is an Indian restaurant near your place in your country, go and have some biryani there now. NOW. You can thank me later!

By Triv.rao (Own work)
(https://commons.wikimedia.org/w/index.php?title=User:Triv.rao)[CC BY-SA 4.0 (http://creativecommons.org/licenses/by-sa/4.0)], via Wikimedia Commons.

13. Drink Milk products (Butter-milk, Lassi,...)

You get many milk-based products in India. One of them is butter-milk. Drinking butter-milk (after mixing it with some salt) helps reduce body heat and compensates for water loss. Lassi is the sweetened version of butter-milk where they add a few other ingredients. If you see a restaurant with 'Lassi' on the sign-board outside, go inside and drink it!

There is also something called curds (yogurt). This is the semi-solid version of butter-milk. You can't drink it, but you can eat it with a spoon. You can also sprinkle some sugar on the top, for taste. Either way, it's tasty and healthy.

You get other flavored milk products like almond-flavored milk (hot, cold), rose milk (cold), etc. These are also very tasty and you should try them at least once while in India.

By Raksanand (Own work) (https://commons.wikimedia.org/w/index.php?title=User:Raksanand) [CC BY-SA 4.0 (http://creativecommons.org/licenses/by-sa/4.0)], via Wikimedia Commons.

14. Drink/Eat Tender Coconut

Tender coconuts are large coconuts with ample water inside them. These are available with small hawkers on the roadside, but it's fine to buy from there. Tender coconut is hygienic as long as the fruit is cut only after you order.

Once you order it, the vendor will cut a tender-coconut from the top and make a small hole. A straw is inserted into this so that you can drink the fresh tender-coconut water (check whether straw is available with the vendor, before ordering). It's cool, healthy and very tasty.

After you finish drinking it, the vendor will cut the tender coconut into two and extract the layer of coconut flesh. This is tastier than the coconut water! Take a spoon along with you, so that you can eat this. You can also eat it with hands or the outer piece of coconut, which the vendor will fashion into a spoon for this purpose.

Ensure that the coconuts are cut in front of you. Do not buy packaged tender-coconut water, as its freshness would have been lost by the time you drink it.

By w:user:PlaneMad (Photo by w:user:PlaneMad) [GFDL (http://www.gnu.org/copyleft/fdl.html), CC-BY-SA-3.0 (http://creativecommons.org/licenses/by-sa/3.0/) or CC BY-SA 2.5-2.0-1.0 (http://creativecommons.org/licenses/by-sa/2.5-2.0-1.0)], via Wikimedia Commons.

15. Buy (and wear) Accessories

Well, buying and learning to wear a saree or kurta is only half the fun. Indians are fond of jewelry and ornaments. There are many accessories that you could wear along with the clothes. For example, you can buy and wear matching bangles (around your wrist), necklaces, earrings, rings, hair pins, hand-bags, shoes, and so on. The list of accessories is actually very long, but the common ones have been mentioned above.

You get accessories in colors and designs you can never imagine. If you have ever had the dream of looking like an Indian Rani (queen), it can be partially fulfilled by wearing all these things, along with saree & shoes (which we will see later). It can be a lot of fun – shopping for accessories and wearing them.

Men have fewer accessories targeted at them - you can get shoes, belts, pouches, sun-glasses, etc., but it's the same like what you get anywhere else. For the traditional wear you can get turbans, pointy shoes, necklaces and watches.

By Harsha K R from Bangalore, India (Her - Part Deux - Engagement Attire) (http://www.flickr.com/people/27526538@N07) [CC BY-SA 2.0 (http://creativecommons.org/licenses/by-sa/2.0)], via Wikimedia Commons.

16. Go for a Lion/Tiger safari

If you are a wildlife enthusiast, you should go for a lion/tiger safari. Both lions and tigers live in India and you can see them in certain national parks and zoos.

Visitor movement maybe restricted in national parks but wildlife tours are organized regularly in many of them. Find out if a national park/jungle safari is available near your place, and go for it.

Lions and Tigers are majestic and stunningly beautiful large carnivorous cats. You can also visit a local zoo to see them. Some zoos offer a safari kind of experience.

Tigers (especially) and lions are being illegally killed in large numbers as their skins are in demand, both in the local market and abroad. Even elephants are killed for ivory. If you come across any products made using them, please do not buy.

Tigers are almost extinct because of this reason. If possible, please create awareness about this problem in your (respective) countries.

By Palvinder (Own work) (https://commons.wikimedia.org/w/index.php?title=User:Palvinder) [CC BY-SA 3.0 (http://creativecommons.org/licenses/by-sa/3.0)], via Wikimedia Commons.

17. Ride an Elephant/Camel

Depending on which part of India you go to, you may be able to ride an elephant or a camel, two of the largest land animals on earth (after giraffe - which you will find in India, but can't ride on). Elephants can be found almost throughout India and camels are restricted to the desert state of Rajasthan and surroundings. You must be accompanied by a trained elephant/camel rider during these rides.

Both elephants and camels have been domesticated in India over many centuries. However, wild elephants (in forests and hilly regions) can be quite dangerous. Don't venture too near if you accidentally come across elephants while traveling.

As mentioned earlier, please do not to buy anything made of ivory as elephants are killed for removing their tusks. If someone tells you of tusks being removed only from dead elephants, most likely it is a lie.

By Saerin (Own work)
(https://commons.wikimedia.org/wiki/User:Saerin) [CC BY-SA 3.0 (http://creativecommons.org/licenses/by-sa/3.0) or GFDL (http://www.gnu.org/copyleft/fdl.html)], via Wikimedia Commons.

18. Buy Jewelery

Gold jewelery is one of the most in-demand items in India. Hence, they are made in all sorts of beautiful designs, shapes & patterns. No other place has the kind of variety that you can find in India. Jewelery goes very well with sarees; there are gold-rings, gold-chains, gold-earrings, etc. Some types of jewelery are worn on the head, some around the waist, some on the wrist, some on the ears, some even on legs. If you attend an Indian wedding, you will find the bride wearing everything mentioned here and probably more!

Some gold jewelery is available for men as well - chain, bracelet or ring. But these are nothing, when compared to the options available for women. The best part about buying gold is its increasing commercial value (with time) and global demand/appeal. Hence, it can be considered as an investment, in a limited sense. The same thing applies for diamond jewelery and you'll find an exhaustive collection of diamond jewelery, as well, in India.

If you don't want to spend a lot of money on gold, you can still buy the (duplicate) designer/imitation jewelery. These look just like gold, but cost very less. You can be assured that the gold plating on them will not disappear, at least until you leave India! :)

By Amitsalla (Own work) (https://commons.wikimedia.org/w/index.php?title=User:Amitsalla) [CC BY 3.0 (http://creativecommons.org/licenses/by/3.0)], via Wikimedia Commons.

19. Attend an Indian wedding

Traditionally, weddings in India are an elaborate affair and they may stretch for a few days in certain localities. You'll be able to find the best of India during weddings. Colors, people, decoration, flowers, entertainment, music, food – everything is extravagant and high quality.

The biggest issue is - as a foreigner, you need to know someone to attend the wedding. But since Indians consider weddings as a show of strength and status, and it is common to see hundreds of people in every wedding ceremony, most Indian families would not mind hosting guests during weddings. All you need to do is - find someone who is going and tag along with them. The easiest way is to take some help from your hotel manager, tour-operator or any friends you might know in India.

By shraddhaphotostories [CC0], via Wikimedia Commons (http://pixabay.com/en/users/shraddhaphotostories/)

20. Eat the Indian bread – Roti/Chapati

The equivalent of western bread is roti, made of wheat. It's called chapati in South/Central India. Roti is a soft, flat (sometimes slightly fluffed) dish that people might have for breakfast, lunch or dinner.

Actually, roti with ghee tastes quite nice, but the real magic is in the sabji (the variety of tasty side-dishes available for roti). Sabji can be made of potato, onion, paneer, peas, mushroom, cauliflower, tomato, etc. It is available with gravy or without. You can also order dhal along with roti – it's a lentil dish; it tastes good and is less spicy.

People may order 1-4 rotis over a single meal, but it's prudent to start with just one. There are a variety of rotis like tandoori-roti, butter-naan, kulcha, parantha (vegetable stuffed roti), etc. The roti/sabji is eaten with one hand. You need to cut a small part of the roti, mix it with a small part of the sabji, put it in your mouth and munch to glory!

By Devika (Flickr: A simple lunch at home) (https://www.flickr.com/people/75531279@N05) [CC BY-SA 2.0 (http://creativecommons.org/licenses/by-sa/2.0)], via Wikimedia Commons.

21. Apply Mehndi

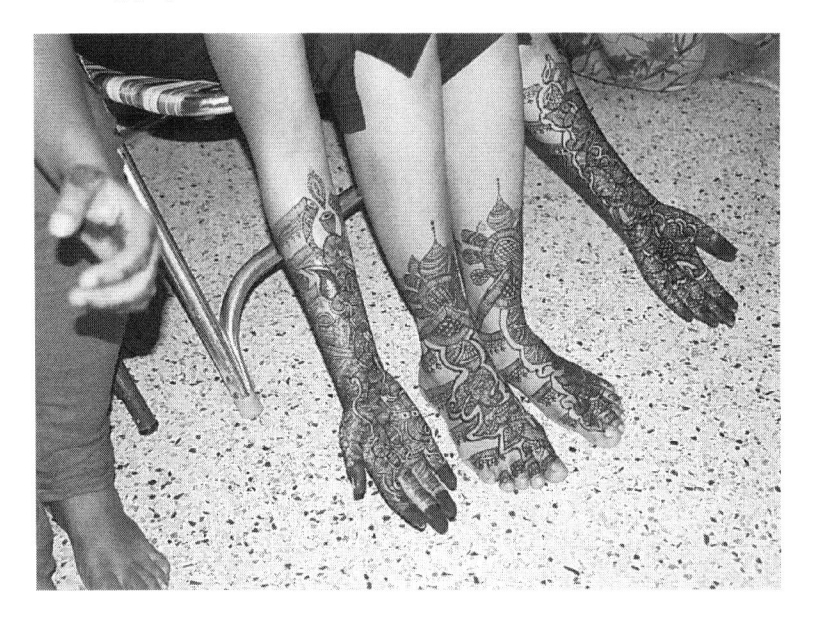

Mehndi or henna is a thick brown paste that is applied in delicate and intricate lines, patterns, and designs, mainly on a woman's hands and legs. Although this is done for beautification purposes now, especially during weddings, it is a practice from ancient Vedic India. Think of it as a temporary, beautiful, feminine tattoo. It is applied mostly by women and children, but sometimes on men also - during marriages, festivals, etc.

You may find professional mehndi artists at a few places. For many Indians, this is mostly applied by friends and relatives, or even by themselves. Be aware that it takes a few hours for the mehndi to dry and form a dark pattern, before you can wash it off. It will be visible for a week or so and then it will automatically fade.

By Nvvchar (Own work)
(https://commons.wikimedia.org/wiki/User:Nvvchar) [CC BY-SA 3.0
(http://creativecommons.org/licenses/by-sa/3.0) or GFDL
(http://www.gnu.org/copyleft/fdl.html)], via Wikimedia Commons.

22. Attend Music Concerts

There are two types of music concerts in India – Classical Music (traditional/devotional songs) and Popular Music (movie and other songs). Ideally, you should try to attend both types of concerts at least once while you are here.

India has a rich tradition of classical music. Among the schools of classical music, Carnatic music is popular in the South & Hindustani is popular in the North. In order to perform in concerts, it's mandatory for the artist to first learn/practice singing or playing a musical instrument for many years. It takes an informed audience with an artistic bent of mind to appreciate the nuances of classical music. However, once immersed in it, this type of music has the power to make you forget everything else. It's divine, graceful and pure.

Thus, Indian classical music is not for everyone. It takes some patience and maturity to enjoy it. If you are not interested in this, you might want to listen to classical-western fusion music, instead of purely classical songs.

Popular music concerts mostly play songs from movies. These are the ones that have a mass appeal. Not every hit song is a dance number. There are so many slow & melodious movie songs that have become well known. Generally, famous singers or music directors conduct such concerts.

You should check the 'events' section/ads in the local newspapers to know about upcoming concerts. You should be able to book tickets online and it is advisable to do so in advance. If a lot of crowd is expected, try to reach the venue a bit earlier.

Tip: If you read, 'A. R. Rehman in concert', just jump and book tickets immediately. He won two Oscars for his music in the movie, 'Slumdog Millionare'. However, he has produced better music/songs for movies in multiple Indian languages. Just look him up on Google or youtube and listen to any song composed by him. His music is magical and he is my favorite composer.

By Tinkubasu (Own work) (https://commons.wikimedia.org/w/index.php?title=User:Tinkubasu) [CC BY-SA 4.0 (http://creativecommons.org/licenses/by-sa/4.0)], via Wikimedia Commons.

23. See Indian Dance

There are many traditional dance-forms in India. Each Indian state has its own form of dance that has been passed on over the centuries. These are classical dances; like the classical music concerts there are classical dance concerts, as well. If you are interested in exploring traditional dance-forms of India, you can go to one of these. They mostly consist of slow and graceful movements, with classical music being played in the background. Some popular classical dance-forms include Bharatnatyam (from Tamil Nadu), Kathakali (from Kerala), Kathak (from North India), etc.

If you want to see loud music and fast dancing, you can see the famous Bollywood 'item numbers'. These are generally part of Bollywood movies and hence when you watch movies, they might be included.

If you want me to recommend some good dance songs - 'Chickni Chameli' (Movie: Agneepath), Kajra re (Movie: Bunty Aur Bubli), Appadi podu (Movie: Gilli), Uyirin uyire (Movie: Kakka Kakka), Mera piya ghar aaya (Movie: Yaraana), Ek do teen (Movie: Tezaab), Lose control (Movie: Rang De Basanti), Bin Tere Sanam [Remix], Aaj ki raat [remix] (Album: Kar le kar le koi dhamaal). Search for these songs on Youtube or music sites and dance to them. They are all good!

By Kamranahmedar (Own work) (https://commons.wikimedia.org/w/index.php?title=User:Kamranahmedar) [CC BY-SA 4.0 (http://creativecommons.org/licenses/by-sa/4.0)], via Wikimedia Commons.

24. Listen to Indian musical instruments

Indian artists have created many unique musical instruments over the centuries and some of them are in use even today. There are instruments like the Veena, Sitar, Tabla, Mrudangam, Sarod, Santoor, and so on that you cannot find anywhere else in the world. Every region/state in India may have its own unique musical instrument. Also, when musicians use familiar instruments like the flute, keyboard, guitar, violin etc. to play Carnatic/Hindustani classical music, it's a great experience.

You can go to music concerts that feature musical instruments (only). These are called 'Instrumental concerts' and you can get info about them from the newspapers/internet. However, the best thing would be to visit a department store selling books/music CDs (in malls, for example) and buy instrumental DVDs. Many music shops will allow you to sample the music before buying it. This way, you can carry Indian music home and listen to it whenever you want. You can also search in Youtube.

India: 55 Must See Places & 50 Must Do Things

By US Government, Public Domain Photo

25. Visit a Heritage house

India's is a very old culture. Even though things are fast changing now, many housekeeping practices, cooking techniques, decoration methods, etc. have been passed on over generations. In some cities, they maintain 'heritage houses' that showcase a traditional Indian house with all its utensils, crockery, decorative items, etc. from the past.

Visiting these sites is an interesting experience. It provides a gateway to the past and showcases the sustainable-living practices of ancient India. Many of these heritage houses are open for public viewing, especially in cities promoting tourism. Just Google 'heritage house + (your city)' or ask your hotel help desk/travel operator for more info.

By Destination8infinity (Own work) (https://commons.wikimedia.org/wiki/User:Destination8infinity) [CC BY-SA 3.0 (http://creativecommons.org/licenses/by-sa/3.0)], via Wikimedia Commons.

26. Get yourself an Ayurvedic Massage/Visit an Ayurvedic Spa

Ayurveda is the name for traditional Indian medicinal practice. Its practitioners use herbs and other naturally available plant ingredients as medicines. Nothing relaxes the body and mind like a traditional Ayurvedic massage/spa. Specially prepared oil is often used, and this will keep you fresh throughout the rest of your journey.

Make sure to double-check the authenticity of the massage parlor you visit and always choose a massage parlor only if it is recommended by trusted sources. Sometimes, illegal activities like prostitution (which is banned in India) can be advertised as massage parlor services. So be careful.

Also, recreational drugs are banned in India. Alcohol

should be available in resorts/large hotels – but don't buy the ones available locally - chances that they are diluted or adulterated are high. It's also advisable not to smoke in public places (it's against the law in a few states/cities).

By Taj Hotels, Resorts and Palaces (Taj images) [CC BY-SA 3.0 (http://creativecommons.org/licenses/by-sa/3.0)], via Wikimedia Commons.

27. Go see a Cricket Match

Indians love cricket. It's similar to baseball, but the ball is pitched on the ground (instead of a full-toss) before a batsman can hit it, and there are two batsmen in the field (instead of four). Well, there are many differences but you'll be able to understand the game if you watch one cricket match on TV before you go to a stadium.

Cricket matches, like football, are about the maddening crowd, energy and noise. Even if you don't understand the game much, you'll still catch some of the enthusiasm and can have a lot of fun in the stadium. Just make sure you read about Sachin Tendulkar and other cricketing greats from India. Some info can be read on espncricinfo.com. You can't possibly feign ignorance about the Cricket God, Sachin Tendulkar, anywhere in India - especially not inside the stadium!

There are three types of cricket matches – 5-day Test matches, 50-over One Day Internationals & T20 (Twenty-

twenty) matches. If you are not from England, Australia, South Africa or other cricket-playing countries, it best to see the shorter version of the game (T20: Twenty-twenty matches). Don't miss the fast/entertaining IPL (Indian Premier League) matches when you are here. You can also watch them on TV.

By Colin Malsingh (Own work) (https://commons.wikimedia.org/w/index.php?title=User:Celidh) [CC BY-SA 3.0 (http://creativecommons.org/licenses/by-sa/3.0)], via Wikimedia Commons.

28. Watch Field Hockey

If you are a big soccer fan, you might find field hockey more interesting than cricket. Field hockey is similar to soccer, but players use hockey sticks to navigate and put the hockey 'puck' into the opponent's nets. The hockey court is smaller and hence the tempo of the game is quick. Field Hockey is the national game of India.

Even though cricket is more popular, hockey matches are conducted regularly and there is an Indian Hockey League. International matches get big crowds (especially matches like India vs Pakistan). All major hockey matches are telecast on sports (TV) channels anyway. Try to catch up with a couple of them.

Badminton, Kabbadi & Chess are other games that are very popular in India.

By Ashlyak (Own work)
(https://commons.wikimedia.org/w/index.php?title=User:Ashlyak) [CC BY-SA

3.0 (http://creativecommons.org/licenses/by-sa/3.0)], via Wikimedia Commons.

29. Learn Yoga/Meditation

Yoga is an ancient exercise-form that is very much relevant today. A healthy mind needs a healthy body, right? If Yoga is exercise for your body, meditation is exercise for your mind! Both Yoga and meditation originated in India. So what better place to learn and practice them?

However, you cannot learn Yoga completely within a few days. You can learn a few basic asanas (exercises) and postures here, and practice after you are back home. You can learn some breathing exercises if the yoga center offers them as well.

A healthy body also needs a healthy mind. Meditation is something you cannot learn but can only practice. Indians consider meditation to be the first step towards self-realization. There are certain places like Auroville (Pondicherry) where many people regularly practice meditation. The process is deceptively simple: You sit in a certain posture, close your eyes and chant something like 'Om' inside your mind. If you do this for 20 minutes everyday, your might feel more relaxed and peaceful inside. Of course, this is a simplistic version; there are entire books on this topic.

By Bhargavinf(Own work)
(https://commons.wikimedia.org/wiki/User:Bhargavinf) [CC BY-SA 3.0 (http://creativecommons.org/licenses/by-sa/3.0)], via Wikimedia Commons.

30. Stick a Bindi on your forehead

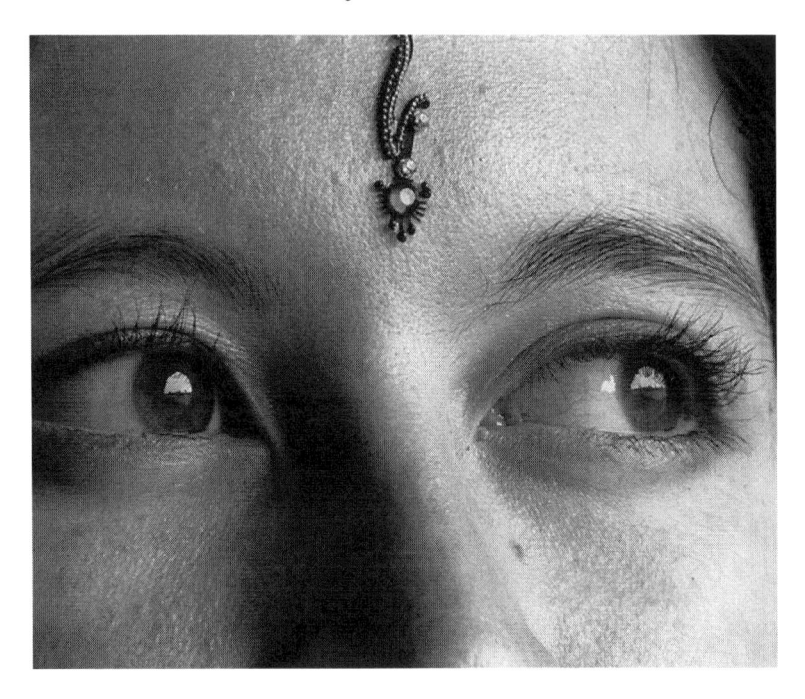

This is for women. A bindi is a small sticker that Indian women apply in the middle their forehead as an accessory, above the eyes. Traditionally it is round in shape and red in color. However, you get a variety of designer bindis (shapes, colors and designs) these days. Stick a designer bindi (matching your dress) to your forehead, while you are in India.

By Drew (http://flickr.com/photos/21253420@N00) [CC BY 2.0 (http://creativecommons.org/licenses/by/2.0)], via Wikimedia Commons.

31. Read books written by Indian authors

Indian authors are not very popular in the world literary scene (except a few), but a lot of English literature is published in India. Whatever your favorite genre, you'll find books in it written by an Indian author in English. Some popular books include,

Book (Author) - Genre

#1. Five Point Someone (Chetan Bhagat) – Fiction, Contemporary.

#2. The God of Small Things (Arundhati Roy) – Fiction, Literary Fiction.

#3. Chanakya's Chant, The Krishna Key (Ashwin Sanghi) – Fiction, Historical Thriller.

#4. The Shiva Triology (Amish Tripathi) - Fiction,

Historical/Mythological Thriller.

#5. I have a Dream, Poor Little Rich Slum (Rashmi Bansal) – Non-Fiction, Social Entrepreneurship.

#6. Wings of Fire (Dr. APJ Abdul Kalam) – Autobiography, Scientist & Former Indian President.

#7. I Dare (Kiran Bedi) – Autobiography, Retired Lady Cop.

#8. From Dongri to Dubai (S Hussain Zaidi) – Non-Fiction, Crime, Mumbai Mafia.

#9. The Room of the Roof, The Flight of the Pigeons, The Blue Umbrella (Ruskin Bond) – Fiction, Literary Fiction.

#10. Malgudi Days, A Bachelor of Arts, The Financial Expert (RK Narayan) – Fiction, Literary Fiction.

#11. Feluda (Sathyajith Ray) – Series, Fiction, Crime/Investigation.

#12. Binodhini (Rabindranath Tagore) - Fiction, Drama/Relationships.

#13. Ladies Coupe (Anita Nair) – Fiction, Women's Fiction.

#14. Jaya – Mahabharata epic retold; Business Sutra – Traditional Indian concepts applied to modern business (Devdutt Pattanaik).

#15. Battle of Bittora (Anuja Chauhan) – Fiction, a love story set in modern Indian politics.

By Narendra Modi (Books presented to the Prime Minister) (https://www.flickr.com/people/92359345@N07) [CC BY-SA 2.0 (http://creativecommons.org/licenses/by-sa/2.0)], via Wikimedia Commons.

32. Ride in an Auto

While there will be call-taxis in every Indian city, hiring an auto to get to any location (within the city/town) is a unique experience. In some towns, an auto might be the only form of transportation. The auto is a three-wheeled mini automobile that is used to ferry passengers from one location to another, for a small price. It is not as big as a car nor as small as a motorcycle. It's somewhere in-between. It's the low-cost version of a taxi.

What makes autos all the more interesting is the chaotic traffic on Indian roads. You can experience the full chaos of Indian roads/transportation system by riding an auto in a busy locality. The way some of the auto-drivers maneuver through the traffic is an art. If you are taking an auto for the first time, it is natural to be slightly worried. It may appear risky, but since these drivers ride the same routes regularly, they can handle it. Try to think of it as a mini adventure-ride in an amusement park :)

You'll find auto stands in street corners or you can stop an empty auto on the main road and instantly board it. In some locations, they run by meter while in others, they run on arbitrary (fixed) price. Don't worry too much if they over-charge you – it will still be less than what you would have paid for a taxi.

A share-auto is a relatively new phenomenon, but I would not recommend it because they pack a lot of people inside the small vehicle. In some places, there are jeeps that are run similarly on shared-basis. A hired auto, however, is yours only.

Since we are on the topic of transportation, public transport (bus/train) is quite easy (and cheap) in India, but use it only during off hours. During peak hours, buses/local trains are overcrowded and it is advisable to avoid them. If you use public transport, carry your belongings with care.

A few small towns still have horse-driven carriages or manually pedaled rickshaws. In Delhi, you can even find electric rickshaws. Depending on your liking, you may want to try these modes of transport once.

By M M from Switzerland (Indien)
(https://www.flickr.com/people/43423301@N07) [CC BY-SA 2.0
(http://creativecommons.org/licenses/by-sa/2.0)], via Wikimedia Commons.

33. Drink the Coffee

If you are in South India, or you happen to visit a South Indian restaurant, ask for 'Filter Coffee'. The filter coffee is the popular Indian version of the coffee that has a strong aroma and excellent taste - it's a brand in itself. If you are a coffee lover, you'll love this!

Cafe Coffee Day is the most popular coffee chain in India, though Starbucks is taking over in the big cities. You will get many varieties of western coffee and some flavors of Indian coffee, here. The best part is, Coffee Day is available in multiple locations at all major Indian cities/towns.

India: 55 Must See Places & 50 Must Do Things

By Charles Haynes (Flickr) (http://flickr.com/photos/87232391@N00) [CC BY-SA 2.0 (http://creativecommons.org/licenses/by-sa/2.0)], via Wikimedia Commons.

34. Read/See the Mythological Epic stories – Ramayana & Mahabharata

Hinduism is the most widespread religion in India and there are two major Hindu mythological epics – Ramayana & Mahabharata. These two are well known across the length and breadth of the country. Though these stories have a religious connection, they are basically interesting situations (set in ancient India) woven together with morals and philosophies.

Try to get a book or a short story version of either Ramayana or Mahabharata and read it. You can also watch movies/videos that are based on either of these epics.

If you want a taste of Indian philosophy, you could read the English translation of the Bhagavad Gita. Note, the content/concepts are quite heavy and even I have not read it fully until now!

These books were written a few thousand years ago and they have been passed from one generation to another, orally and in written form. Many parts of them are still hugely applicable in our contemporary times.

By Booradleyp1 (Own work)
(https://commons.wikimedia.org/wiki/User:Booradleyp1) [CC BY-SA 3.0 (http://creativecommons.org/licenses/by-sa/3.0)], via Wikimedia Commons.

35. Sponsor a meal in an orphanage and interact with the kids

India is a huge country (1.2 billion people) and many people live below the poverty line. Social security schemes designed by the Government do not fully reach the beneficiaries. Due to these reasons (and many more), kids may be abandoned or uncared for by their parents. Many such kids are brought up in centers across the country and these organizations mostly depend on private donations.

Orphanages have many schemes that allow people to donate money or things in kind. You could look at donating meals to kids for a day (for example). On that day, you'll generally be allowed to visit the kids and interact with them. Since they come from tough backgrounds, they will be very happy to see you!

By Indian Navy (http://www.indiannavy.nic.in/news-events/womens-day-enc) [CC BY 2.5 in (http://creativecommons.org/licenses/by/2.5/in/deed.en) or CC BY 2.5 in (http://creativecommons.org/licenses/by/2.5/in/deed.en)], via Wikimedia Commons.

36. Have an Astrologer predict your future

In India, many people have a strong belief in destiny and astrology. The first thing most people do when a child is born in a family is getting his/her horoscope written. People believe that the orientation of the planets and stars (which is used in preparing the horoscope) has a role to play in the child's future. Many marriages (arranged by the family) are later fixed based on horoscope compatibility.

There are different schools of astrology. One such school uses the lines on your hand to predict the future (in very generic terms). It's known as palmistry in the world, but I am not sure if both of them use the same criteria for predictions.

Anyway, if someone you can trust recommends a good astrologer, do visit and get your hands read by them. There is a chance that certain events in your future might be predicted accurately! Astrologers charge very less for individual hand readings. However, do check the price before you approach them.

Be careful about remedies they might offer, especially if it involves money. Good astrologers don't offer remedies. There are a lot of unscrupulous astrologers trying to make a quick buck out there. That's why you should approach an astrologer through recommendation. Even then, just listen to what they say about you/your future, and forget it once you walk out. These may become memories to cherish, later on. Take someone who can translate the readings if language is going to be a hurdle.

By Wellcome Images (http://wellcomeimages.org/) [CC BY 4.0 (http://creativecommons.org/licenses/by/4.0)], via Wikimedia Commons.

37. Participate in Indian festivals

Like weddings, Indians celebrate festivals with a lot of pomp and enthusiasm. One popular festival that is celebrated across India is Deepavali or Diwali – the festival of lights. The whole of India will be bursting crackers, lighting lamps, eating sweets and generally having a nice time on this day. Walking on the streets will be a deafening experience with all kind of crackers being burst during the morning, and skies will be lighted by rockets and sparkly firecrackers during the evenings.

There are many other, regional festivals like Holi (during which people splash color powder/color water on everyone, including strangers), Ganesh Chaturthi, Navratri, Durga Pooja, Krishna Jayanthi, Karthigai Deepam, Golu, etc. Each of these festivals is celebrated in a unique way. The best thing is to find out which festival is happening around your locality during your visit and attend or participate in the celebrations.

By Sriram Jagannathan (Flickr: Chennai diwali) (https://www.flickr.com/people/61089525@N04) [CC BY 2.0

India: 55 Must See Places & 50 Must Do Things *(http://creativecommons.org/licenses/by/2.0)], via Wikimedia Commons.*

38. Drink Lime Soda/Masala Soda

Lemonade is a much-loved drink all over the world. You'll find fresh lime-juice across India too. However, two specialty drinks available in India are Lime soda and Masala soda.

Lime soda is made of mixing bottled soda water with lime+sugar (or) lime+sugar+salt (or) lime+salt. These days, there are many packaged lime-sodas as well. Masala soda is quite unique; it is made by mixing bottled soda water with spices. This drink is not sweet, but it is very interesting and refreshing. Masala soda is not available everywhere - if you find it, try it.

Statutory warning: Check if the shopkeeper uses branded bottled soda and not spurious ones.

By Siddhantsahni28 (Own work)
(https://commons.wikimedia.org/w/index.php?title=User:Siddhantsahni28)

[CC BY-SA 4.0 (http://creativecommons.org/licenses/by-sa/4.0)], via Wikimedia Commons.

39. See a Peacock

The peacock is the national bird of India. It is one of the most beautiful and largest birds of the world. The beauty of its feathers is legendary - especially when it spreads them out during mating time into a huge formation. People wait for hours together to see a peacock spread its feathers. Some species of peacocks are totally white and these are interesting to see, as well. You will find peacocks in every major zoo/park in India. If you are lucky, you might even find a few during a forest or trekking trip.

By Pep1863 (Own work)
(https://commons.wikimedia.org/wiki/User:Pep1863) [CC0], via Wikimedia Commons.

40. Watch domestic animals share the road

In India, you are usually never walking/driving alone on any road. This is because you will also find animals like dogs, cats, cows, buffaloes, camels and sometimes, even elephants on the road. It's an interesting sight to watch a herd of goats/buffaloes walk on the road while people patiently wait for them to cross. This is also a reason why over-speeding is not a practical option on Indian roads - one never knows who or what might come in between!

By Sumeet Jain from San Francisco, USA (12/16/07 12:27 AM) (http://www.flickr.com/people/73953412@N00) [CC BY-SA 2.0 (http://creativecommons.org/licenses/by-sa/2.0)], via Wikimedia Commons.

41. Take a Tour of the slums

Slums are the residential colonies of the under-privileged people and migrant workers. A lot of people live in cramped tent-like houses in slums located in and around large cities.

Personally, this would not be my favorite activity. I find the concept of slum tours shocking, not interesting. However, slum tours are quite common and tourists do visit them. I guess the popularity of the movie, 'Slumdog Millionaire' has inspired a lot of people to visit slums and see the living conditions for themselves. These days, a lot of development programs are being implemented in slums.

While slum tours are not positively exciting, they might encourage you to be thankful to what you already have and admire the grit/determination of people who are fighting on a daily basis to improve their living conditions.

By Nishantd85 (Own work) (https://commons.wikimedia.org/w/index.php?title=User:Nishantd85) [CC BY-SA 3.0 (http://creativecommons.org/licenses/by-sa/3.0)], via Wikimedia Commons.

42. Visit the Palaces & Forts

Indian palaces are very different from palaces elsewhere. Before Independence, India was a collection of large number of princely states. Since kingdoms existed until the middle of twentieth century, there are many palaces and forts in India where royal families lived or continue to live.

Many palaces in India are open to public viewing and one can find all the articles, weapons, etc. used by the royal families earlier, on display. Some of these palaces and forts will blow you away by their grandeur and luxury.

There are also some famous hotels built to resemble a palace, while some companies have converted an existing palace into a hotel. Staying in a hotel like this could be a great way to experience what living in a palace used to be like in India.

By Birsa Murmu (Own work)
(https://commons.wikimedia.org/w/index.php?title=User:Birsa.murmu) [CC BY-SA 3.0 (http://creativecommons.org/licenses/by-sa/3.0)], via Wikimedia Commons.

43. Explore the Colonial Heritage structures

India was ruled by the British for over 100 years. During this time, the British (and other Europeans) built a lot of buildings and structures that had a mix of Indian and European architecture. Many of these structures and buildings (like churches, public halls, administrative premises, etc.) are being preserved as heritage sites. Some of them have been converted into universities, museums, administrative premises, Government offices, etc. You can find and visit these colonial heritage structures in every major Indian city.

By Yoga Balaji (File:Chennai High Court.jpg) (https://commons.wikimedia.org/wiki/File%3AChennai_High_Court_1200x80 0.jpg) [CC BY-SA 3.0 (http://creativecommons.org/licenses/by-sa/3.0)], via Wikimedia Commons.

44. Visit the Beaches

Most of the beaches in India are meant for families to gather and relax. Kids love to play on the sand while adults can relax over soothing breeze and fiddling waves. The best time to visit a beach would be early mornings (to view the sunrise in the east) or late evenings (to view the sunset in the west). Of course, any time is a good time to visit beaches in India, except late nights and hot afternoons.

Since Indian beaches are home to families, various recreational activities/eateries throng them. You can shoot balloons, take a horse-ride, take a picture standing next to (duplicate) Indian actors/actresses, etc. You can eat many snack items like bajji, vada, chaat, popcorn, raw/ripe mango & pineapple pieces, cucumber (with salt+chilli powder) or sundal (boiled-peas) with raw-mango pieces. You can also lie down on the sand or splash in the water.

By Darshan Simha (Marina Beach)
(https://www.flickr.com/people/91419861@N03) [CC BY 2.0

(http://creativecommons.org/licenses/by/2.0)], via Wikimedia Commons.

45. Visit Art Galleries

Indian art is very different from western art, especially when it is based on Indian landscapes, objects, and people. As lively colors are an everyday obsession in India, it is natural for art works to follow its real-life inspiration.

Both Government art galleries and private ones are available in cities and tourist locations. Art has not been commercialized much in India - hence, you might get some excellent works for a low price. In a few galleries, you can also negotiate to get a better price. Even if you don't want to buy the art, just visiting the galleries to admire the work is a good way to spend a day immersed in Indian culture.

[Public domain], via Wikimedia Commons.
(https://commons.wikimedia.org/wiki/File:Celebrations_of_Krishna%E2%80%99s_birth_-_Google_Art_Project.jpg)

46. Learn to Cook Indian food

The cuisine in India is often focused on vegetarian dishes. There are many communities in India who don't eat meat and this practice has been passed on over many generations. Whether it is vegetarian or non-vegetarian food, however, the variety of dishes available in India is mind-boggling.

Cooking in India can therefore be a complex process as it involves multiple grains, spices, and vegetables. Identifying the basic ingredients requires some hand holding. If you stay with an Indian family, you can easily learn the basics of Indian cooking. Thereupon, you can prepare your own dishes with the help of cookbooks, videos, etc.

While we are on the topic of cooking, I should mention a word about vegetables. In India, you can find various types of vegetables available in the market and many of them are commonly used for cooking. Even if you don't get a chance to cook each of them, make sure you sample them in homes or restaurants.

By Top left and Top right: Argenberg (Vyacheslav Argenberg, Creative Commons Attribution 2.0) and Bottom: mynameisharsha (Harsha K R, Creative Commons Attribution ShareAlike 2.0) I'm checking the former attribution below for all three on the assumption that it is the more general one. [CC BY-SA 2.0 (http://creativecommons.org/licenses/by-sa/2.0)], via Wikimedia Commons. [https://www.flickr.com/photos/argenberg/, https://www.flickr.com/photos/mynameisharsha/]

47. Learn an Indian language

India, like many other countries, is divided into different states. However, unlike other countries, people of each Indian state speak a different language. According to a census conducted in 2001, there are at least 30 major languages that are spoken by more than 1 million native speakers, each. Most of these languages also have their own script.

Five languages have been granted the classical language status by the Government of India (GoI). They are: Sanskrit, Tamil, Kannada, Telugu & Pali. This status basically means that these languages are very old, have a different spoken/written version, etc. Unofficially, there are many more languages that adhere to the classical language terms.

Hindi is the most popular and widely-spoken language in India. It is also the national language. If you want to learn one language that will enable you to communicate with people in most states/cities, this is the one. Learning a language takes many years, but you can equip yourself with basic and important words, sentence formation, script, etc. It will help especially if you travel to the interiors of the country.

Sanskrit was the ancient language of India (though not commonly used anymore) and it is considered to be on par with Greek, Latin, and other old languages. Many other languages, like Hindi and Urdu, stem from it; ancient texts in India were written in Sanskrit and some of them have survived until today. Since the British ruled India for many years, English is a very common language as well. It is also one of the official languages of India along with Hindi. English is the medium of education in most big towns and cities. Even otherwise, children learn basic English. The language used in most signboards, direction boards, public places, shops, products etc. is mostly English (along with local languages).

You can find various self-learning aids/courses, both online and in coaching centers, in India and abroad. You may also find many books like "Learn Hindi through English in 30 days", etc. You can pick up one of these to learn the basics.

By Arjunaraoc (Own work) (https://commons.wikimedia.org/wiki/User:Arjunaraoc) [CC BY-SA 3.0 (http://creativecommons.org/licenses/by-sa/3.0)], via Wikimedia Commons.

48. Indulge in Spiritualism

India is the birthplace of many major religions including Hinduism, Buddhism, Jainism, and Sikhism. One of the ultimate goals of any religion is self-realization. Whether it is a two-minute prayer in a temple, a many-hour meditation or a two-week stay in an ashram renouncing all worldly pleasures, you are sure to experience spirituality here. A change that enables you to assess yourself more truthfully, make decisions with clarity & peace of mind is often the result of becoming spiritual.

All that said, spiritualism is also a huge business in some parts of India. For every authentic and successful guru, you are bound to find at least ten fake ones. This is the reason why it is important to verify the credentials of the organization before you get involved in any spiritual activity. If a spiritual organization is openly commercial or is 'selling' something in a pushy manner, it may be better to avoid them.

India: 55 Must See Places & 50 Must Do Things

By Mefodiyz (Own work)
(https://commons.wikimedia.org/wiki/User:Mefodiyz) [CC BY-SA 3.0
(http://creativecommons.org/licenses/by-sa/3.0)], via Wikimedia Commons.

49. Rural Tourism

The real backbone and spirit of India is its villages. Living in villages is very different and in many ways, challenging. You'll wonder how people with such less material wealth manage to be so happy. You'll wonder how easy sustainable-living is, and how people have been practicing its principles in India for centuries together.

Rural tourism is a relatively new concept, like the home-stay. If you are able to arrange your stay in a village, in someone's house, don't miss the chance. You can even try your hand at farming, animal rearing, star gazing, Temple festivities, and so on while there.

By Abhijit Kar Gupta (Flickr: Sunrise time at my village) (https://www.flickr.com/people/31518092@N04) [CC BY 2.0 (http://creativecommons.org/licenses/by/2.0)], via Wikimedia Commons.

50. Read Indian Blogs

http://www.hoteldepot.in/blog/travel/30-top-travel-blogs-in-india-in-2013/

The above link lists 30 good travel blogs in India. There are many more blogs/sites that will help you identify interesting locations and plan your travel in India, and they are all available online. Guides by Lonely Planet and others, information given by travel agents, etc. can also be helpful.

I welcome you to visit my blog - http://www.destinationinfinity.org as well. This is more of a personal blog and I write on many topics, including travel stories.

By the way, if you happen to visit my city (Chennai), please do drop me a line using the contact-form page of my blog. I'll be more than glad to catch up with you over a cup of coffee, if I am available.

List of Recommended Services

List of Recommended Services for Tourists Visiting India

Five good e-commerce websites/apps:

1. Flipkart – www.flipkart.com
2. Amazon India – www.amazon.in
3. Snapdeal – www.snapdeal.com
4. Home Shop 18 – www.homeshop18.com
5. Infibeam – www.infibeam.com

Five good travel and hotel booking websites/apps:

1. Make My Trip – www.makemytrip.com
2. Clear Trip – www.cleartrip.com
3. Trip Advisor – www.tripadvisor.in
4. Yatra – www.yatra.com
5. Go Ibibo – www.goibibo.com

Four good taxi booking websites/apps:

1. Ola – www.olacabs.com (Taxi & Auto)
2. Meru – www.merucabs.com
3. Uber – www.uber.com
4. Taxi For Sure – www.taxiforsure.com

Indian Railways official ticket booking website:

IRCTC – www.irctc.co.in

National Portal of India:

www.india.gov.in

Ministry of Tourism, Govt. Of India:

www.tourism.gov.in

Seven good Indian Cellular/3g-4g Internet service providers:

1. Airtel – www.airtel.in
2. Vodafone – www.vodafone.in
3. Idea Cellular - www.ideacellular.com
4. Aircel – www.aircel.com
5. Reliance – www.rcom.co.in
6. BSNL – www.bsnl.co.in
7. Tata Docomo – www.tatadocomo.com

Five good Tourist Operators:

1. Thomas Cook – www.thomascook.in
2. Cox and Kings - www.coxandkings.com
3. SITA World Tours – www.sitatours.com
4. Kesari – www.kesari.in
5. SOTC – www.sotc.in

Two good Movie booking websites:

1. Book my show – www.in.bookmyshow.com
2. Ticket New – www.ticketnew.com

Five good Newspapers in India:

1. The Hindu – www.thehindu.com
2. Hindustan Times – www.hindustantimes.com

3. DNA India – www.dnaindia.com
4. Times of India – www.timesofindia.com
5. First Post – www.firstpost.com

Four good English Magazines in India:

1. India Today – www.indiatoday.intoday.in
2. Outlook – www.outlookindia.com
3. Frontline – www.frontline.in
4. Readers Digest India – www.readersdigest.co.in

Four good Social Networks in India:

1. Facebook
2. WhatsApp
3. Twitter
4. Instagram

Six good Mineral Water brands in India:

1. Kinley
2. Aquafina
3. Bisleri
4. Bailey's
5. Himalayan
6. Tata Water Plus

Four good Music streaming sites in India:

1. Gaana - www.gaana.com
2. Hungama – www.hungama.com
3. Saavn – www.saavn.com
4. Wynk – www.wynk.in

Four good Classifieds sites in India:

1. OLX – www.olx.in
2. Quikr – www.quikr.com
3. Just Dial – www.justdial.com (Web & Phone)
4. Free Ads – www.freeads.in (Web & Print)

Emergency phone numbers in India:

1. Police – 100
2. Fire – 101
3. Ambulance – 102
4. Emergency disaster management – 108

Printed in Great Britain
by Amazon